healthy eating:
# the prostate care cookbook

Professor Margaret Rayman,
Kay Dilley and Kay Gibbons

**Prostate**Research
PROSTATE CANCER RESEARCH FOUNDATION

# healthy eating:
# the prostate
# care cookbook

Photography by Will Heap

Kyle Cathie Limited

First published in Great Britain in 2009 by
Kyle Cathie Limited
122 Arlington Road
London NW1 7HP
general.enquiries@kyle-cathie.com
www.kylecathie.com

ISBN 978 1 85626 869 1

Editor Katharina Hahn
Editorial assistant Vicki Murrell
Designer Arno Devo
Photographer Will Heap
Proofreader Anne Newman
Indexer Alex Corrin
Home economist and stylist
Annie Nichols
Production Lisa Pinnell, Gemma John

Colour reproduction by Sang Choy
Printed in Singapore by Star Standard

# contents

# acknowledgements

Our grateful thanks go to celebrity chefs Raymond Blanc, Gino D'Acampo, Alex Mackay, Cyrus Todiwala and Antony Worrall Thompson for providing us with some wonderful recipes. Particular thanks go to John Walter, Head Chef at the University of Surrey's Lakeside Restaurant, who searched his repertoire for dishes to fulfil our rigorous criteria, and to Dr John Rayman who tried and tested many recipes and contributed a number of his own.

We are also most grateful for the expert help provided by Professor Peter Bramley (lycopene), Professor Mike Clifford (polyphenols), Dr Jonathan Brown (phytoestrogens), Dr Albena Dinkova-Kostova (cruciferous vegetables) and Dr John Lodge (vitamin E) who checked the scientific text for accuracy and to Dr Elina Hyppönen and Professor Joe Millward who gave helpful advice on vitamin D.

Last but not least, we would like to thank our friends and families who both provided recipes and supported and encouraged us throughout this very demanding project.

# foreword by the PCRF

The Prostate Cancer Research Foundation (PCRF) has two aims: first, to promote independent worldwide research into all aspects of prostate cancer, and second, to share the crucial knowledge gathered from that research via our Forum which is attended by the world's top prostate cancer experts.

Our objectives are:
* To fund research that helps to find the cure for prostate cancer.
* To fund research that contributes to finding the causes of prostate cancer.
* To fund the best quality research.
* To fund research that offers better outcomes to men who are diagnosed with prostate cancer.
* To enable prostate cancer specialists to share information on a regular basis.

**Why Research is so important**
Prostate cancer is the most common cancer in men in the UK, representing a quarter of all new cases of cancer diagnosed. It is the second-most common cause of cancer death in UK men, with 10,000 men a year dying from it – that's one man every hour.

More research into the disease is needed, as there is still so much we do not know. For example, we do not know why the prostate enlarges in a benign manner as men grow older. We do not have an accurate test that differentiates between cancers that need urgent treatment and those cancers that may never need treating. Funding for research into prostate cancer is significantly less than for other common cancers, but the need is greater than ever as the incidence is estimated to increase sharply as our population ages.

The PCRF has been proud to support Prof Rayman since 2004, when we first funded her project to investigate the effects of selenium intake and its ability to reduce the incidence of prostate cancer. This initial research has led to the development of this cookbook.

Evidence clearly points to diet as a significant factor in the development of prostate cancer, and several studies have reported increased prostate cancer in populations that have switched from their traditional diet to a Western one. However, despite these instances there has never been a study to combine all the published research on diet and the implications for prostate cancer development. This cookbook is a unique and valuable resource for men and their families who would like to put these findings to practical use and help in maintaining a healthy prostate. The recipes included in this book by Prof Rayman and her team can help men understand the types of foods that may be beneficial, and in what quantities.

We are very pleased to be able to support this cookbook and we know it will become a very valuable resource for men, and for those who care about them, to help improve the health of their prostates.

Bon Appetit!

Dr Chris Adams, Chairman
Professor Christopher Woodhouse, Scientific Chairman

ProstateResearch
PROSTATE CANCER RESEARCH FOUNDATION

# introduction

Rarely a day passes without new claims being made of the beneficial or harmful effects of diet on health and disease. The claims made for prostate cancer are no exception. There is growing scientific evidence that strongly suggests that diets rich in certain foods can help prevent this disease or its spread. There is also evidence to indicate a harmful effect of other foods. Prostate cancer is often slow to develop and spread and so strategies that can influence its progression have considerable potential. For those living with the condition, a controlled diet may provide the only means of active treatment. But it can be hard to interpret the evidence and put it into practice. Here we have untangled the scientific jargon and put all the information into one place to enable you to benefit from this research. By simply following our recommendations and including some of these tried and tested recipes in your diet, you could improve the health of your prostate.

## The scale of the prostate cancer problem

Thirty-five thousand new diagnoses each year make prostate cancer the most common cancer to affect men in the UK. In fact, around 80 per cent of UK men have evidence of prostate cancer at post-mortem examination although it accounts for only 12 per cent of male cancer deaths. Prostate cancer has become more common over the last two decades, though this is partly due to more widespread screening and improved detection techniques. On a global scale, prostate cancer is the second-most common cancer after lung cancer; over 670,000 diagnoses are made each year. The numbers vary greatly between countries, with the highest rates reported in the US and Sweden, and the lowest in Japan, India and China. This reported variation may also be partly due to differences in the availability of screening and detection techniques, but it is widely accepted that at least some of it is due to differences in diet.

## What are the risk factors?

The causes of prostate cancer are not fully understood, but there are several known risk factors, the greatest of which is age, with risk increasing rapidly from 50 onwards. The existence of prostate cancer or breast cancer in an immediate family member also increases risk. Men of African-American descent appear to have an increased risk while men of Asian descent have a lower risk. These risk factors cannot be modified. There is, however, a growing body of evidence to show that there is a major risk factor which can be modified – that of diet.

## Diet – a modifiable risk factor

The link between diet and prostate cancer is reflected in the low disease rates in Asian countries where diets are low in meat and saturated fats, and high in plant foods, fibre and fish. This contrasts with the high rates in Western countries where diets are rich in meat and fat and low in plant foods. When people migrate from an Asian country to a Western country and adopt the diet and lifestyle of that country, their risk of prostate cancer increases. Furthermore, the incidence of cancer in Asia is increasing with Westernisation. This strengthens the theory that development of prostate cancer is affected by environmental factors, the most important of which is probably diet. There are several nutrients and foods which research shows may be able to influence the risk of prostate cancer development and progression, making dietary modification a useful and accessible strategy. It is important to remember, however, that research in all these areas is ongoing and the picture may well change as more information becomes available.

## How can foods and nutrients affect the risk of prostate cancer development and progression?

Research has shown that some nutrients and food components can act through one or a combination of the mechanisms summarised below to reduce the risk and spread of cancer. A full explanation of these mechanisms can be found in the Second Expert Report of the World Cancer Research Fund American Institute for Cancer Research 'Food, Nutrition, Physical Activity and the Prevention of Cancer: a Global Perspective' which can be accessed on www.dietandcancerreport.org.

Some foods or nutrients may:
* behave as antioxidants, reducing oxidative stress that can damage cells and molecules
* reduce inflammation which is associated with a higher risk of cancer

* improve the immune response, helping the body fight cancer
* prevent damage to DNA or help its repair
* halt the growth of prostate cancer cells
* cause prostate cancer cells to die
* reduce the invasion of tumour cells into the surrounding tissue
* prevent the formation of new blood vessels in the tumour, reducing its ability to grow
* change the behaviour of genes so that protective genes can act efficiently
* increase the rate at which compounds that can cause cancer can be detoxified and removed from the body
* modify the behaviour of hormones or their receptors, most notably by reducing the activation of the androgen receptor which can reduce prostate cancer risk.

*(See Glossary on page 170 for explanation of terms used)*

## Identifying the relevant foods and the quantities required

Through extensive reading of the published literature on the topic, we have identified foods and nutrients that have been linked to prostate cancer, both beneficially and detrimentally. These foods and food components are listed in the table below. The evidence for each of these foods and nutrients is discussed separately in the following pages. Research is ongoing but the most convincing evidence is probably that for lycopene/tomatoes and selenium.

Evidence for an effect of these foods is provided by studies carried out on human populations. In these studies, intakes of the food in question or levels in the blood are recorded within a population group and compared to rates of prostate cancer. In this way it is possible to identify whether high intakes of a certain food are associated with an increased or decreased risk.

Further evidence can be seen in animal studies, but it is hard to draw direct comparisons with humans. Finally, interesting observations have been made in laboratory experiments where food components or nutrients have been added to prostate cancer cells. These studies provide an insight into the effects of each food component.

For each food or food component identified, we endeavoured to establish the quantity required in the diet for a noticeable effect. Based on this, and taking into account a realistic level of intake, we have made recommendations for consumption or limitation in the diet. Quantitative guidelines have been given where possible.

To help increase intake and meet these guidelines, we have selected recipes that are rich in the foods and nutrients believed to be beneficial for protecting against prostate cancer. For each recipe we have indicated which beneficial foods or nutrients are well represented in that dish; see 'good source of' for substantial amounts and 'source of' for smaller but significant amounts. In setting these measures we have considered the number of times per day that a food is likely to be eaten, as well as the amount that is realistic to use in a recipe. For further information, the approximate calorie, fat and saturated fat content of each portion has also been included.

### Taking control
In addition to the potential physical benefits of changing your diet, using this recipe book may have psychological benefits. Consciously

| Foods and nutrients linked with a beneficial or detrimental effect on prostate cancer risk | |
|---|---|
| **Beneficial** | **Detrimental** |
| *Allium* vegetables | Burnt or overcooked meat |
| Cruciferous vegetables | Dairy products |
| Fish | Fat and saturated fat |
| Tomatoes/Lycopene | |
| Phytoestrogens | |
| Polyphenols | |
| Selenium | |
| Vitamin D? | |
| Vitamin E | |

making changes to your diet and lifestyle is associated with a positive, optimistic attitude and a feeling of being in control. This has long been known to improve the immune system and can therefore have a direct effect on how your disease progresses. Men with an increasing PSA level after primary treatment who attended a series of dietary and cooking classes were able to make a change to a prostate-healthy diet that emphasised plant-based foods and fish. Three months later their PSA doubling time had lengthened and quality of life had improved. We hope that this book will empower many men and their families to be active participants in influencing the outcome of their disease.

## One last word

While the evidence for an effect of many of these foods on prostate cancer risk or spread, when taken separately, may be inconclusive, when taken together their effect may be significant. Food components can interact so that the effect they have together is more than the sum of their individual effects; for instance components of soya can intensify the ability of vitamin D to slow the growth of prostate cancer cells. With that in mind, even if you cannot achieve the full recommendations, we encourage you to attempt as many of the suggested modifications to your diet as possible.

# *allium* vegetables

*Allium* vegetables are bulbous plants that have a distinctive taste and odour that make them ideal for use in cooking. Commonly eaten *Allium* vegetables include garlic, onion, spring onions (scallions), shallots, leeks and chives. Some research suggests that men who eat a diet rich in these foods have a lower risk of developing prostate cancer.

The taste and odour of *Allium* vegetables comes from a group of organosulphur compounds. These are formed during the natural ageing process of the plant or from the activity of an enzyme called alliinase that is released when the plant is chopped or crushed. It is these compounds that have been identified as having anti-cancer properties. It is important to note, however, as shown with garlic, that the heat of cooking can destroy alliinase activity, preventing the formation of the active anti-cancer compounds. However, if garlic is left to stand for 10 minutes after cutting or crushing, the alliinase has time to do its work and the active allyl sulphur compounds are formed.

### Evidence from human studies
Garlic is the *Allium* vegetable most commonly described in research studies as having anti-cancer properties. A small Turkish study demonstrated a reduction in PSA level in nine patients with prostate cancer after they had taken a liquid garlic extract for a period of one month. The average PSA level of these men fell from 8.9 to 3.6ng/ml and the fall was accompanied by an improvement in symptoms.

A study carried out in Shanghai investigated the effect of intake of *Allium* vegetables, including garlic, spring onions, onions, chives and leeks, on the risk of prostate cancer in 238 men with confirmed prostate cancer and 471 healthy men for comparison. Results showed that men who ate more than 10g of *Allium* vegetables per day were 49 per cent less likely to develop prostate cancer than those who ate less than 2.2g per day. When vegetables were considered individually, men who ate more than 2.1g of garlic or scallions (spring onions) per day reduced their risk of developing the disease by 53 per cent (garlic) and 70 per cent (spring onions) compared to those who did not eat garlic or spring onions at all.

While some studies have seen a protective association between *Allium* vegetables and the risk of prostate cancer, others have seen none. This may be partly due to the varied types and concentrations of organosulphur compounds but may also reflect the fact that formation of the active compounds takes time to occur and is prevented if the vegetables are cooked straight after preparation. *Allium* vegetables are also often served with other foods, such as tomatoes, that have been identified as having anti-cancer properties so the effect may be from the combination rather than from one type of vegetable alone.

### The effect of *Allium* vegetables

*Allium* vegetables or their products e.g. diallyl disulphide (DADS) are reported to suppress the activation of cancer-causing compounds, increase the action of enzymes that detoxify cancer-causing compounds, prevent the growth of new blood vessels that are required for the tumour to grow, suppress cancer cell division, cause the death of cancer cells, decrease DNA damage and reduce the response to androgen. They have also been shown to help reduce inflammation, a feature associated with many cancers.

Other components of garlic and onion besides organosulphur compounds are said to have cancer-preventive effects. For instance, garlic is a source of the amino acid arginine which may help to reduce inflammation, while onions are a source of the polyphenol, quercetin, which can help prevent cancer-cell growth.

### What quantity of *Allium* vegetables do we eat?

The quantities of onion and garlic consumed by population groups in ten European countries were reported by the European Prospective Investigation into Cancer and Nutrition (EPIC) in 2002. Men in Greece were reported to eat the largest amount of onions and garlic with an average daily intake of over 28g, while men in Germany were reported to eat the least, with an average daily serving of less than 8g. The average intake of onion and garlic by the general population of the UK is reported as being less than 10g per day with only 15 per cent of British males eating 6g (about 2 cloves) or more of garlic per week, compared to 46 per cent of Shanghai men.

The average use of onions in America was reported by the United States Department of Agriculture (USDA) as being 21.6lb per person per year in 2006 (equivalent to about 27g per day). The USDA also reported that the American demand for garlic had increased during the 1990s along with greater awareness of its potential health benefits. Garlic use in 2008 was estimated as 3lb per person, equivalent to about 3.7g per day which was more than double the use recorded in 1990.

### Other benefits and risks of *Allium* vegetables

Other health benefits attributed to garlic and onions include protection against microbial infections and the reduction of risk factors for cardiovascular disease. While *Allium* vegetables are generally safe to consume, it should be noted that garlic is known to have a thinning effect on blood and can interfere with some prescription drugs.

### Recommendations

The current UK guideline for fruit and vegetable consumption is at least five 80g portions per day. In the US 2–2½ cups of vegetables per day are recommended. Although there are no specific guidelines for the consumption of *Allium* vegetables, the World Health Organization (WHO) suggests 2–5g (approximately one clove) of fresh garlic per day for

general health promotion in adults. We suggest that you consume *Allium* vegetables, particularly garlic, several times per week. Don't forget that garlic should be left to stand for about 10 minutes after crushing or chopping before cooking to allow the anti-cancer compounds time to form.

The summary table below left details the quantities of *Allium* vegetables associated with beneficial effects, as well as our suggested target intake and our definition of a 'good source of' and 'source of' that have been included in the recipes in the book.

## Allium Vegetables

| | |
|---|---|
| **Effects seen at...** (depending on the study) | Greater than 10g of *Allium* vegetables per day *or* greater than 2.1g of garlic or spring onions (scallions) per day |
| **Target intake...** | 3 or more garlic cloves per week *or* 3 or more servings of 80g *Allium* vegetables per week |
| **Good source of...** | 1 clove of garlic 80g *Allium* vegetables |
| **Source of...** | ¼ clove of garlic 20g *Allium* vegetables |

# cruciferous vegetables

Cruciferous vegetables are edible plants from the *Cruciferae (Brassicaceae)* family that take their name from their flower which has four petals in a cross-like shape. The most commonly eaten cruciferous vegetables are listed below:

* Broccoli
* Cauliflower
* Cabbage
* Brussels sprouts
* Bok choy (Pak choi)
* Rocket
* Watercress
* Collard
* Kale
* Radish
* Turnip
* Garden cress
* Mustard
* Swede
* Horseradish
* Wasabi

All cruciferous vegetables contain compounds known as glucosinolates. When the vegetables are bruised, chopped or chewed, the enzyme myrosinase is released from the broken cells and reacts with the glucosinolates to form compounds known as isothiocyanates and indoles. It is these sulphur-containing compounds that are responsible for the sometimes pungent aroma and spicy taste of these vegetables. More importantly,

they are biologically active and have been identified as having anti-cancer properties.

Because the activity of myrosinase is destroyed on heating, cooking can prevent the conversion of glucosinolates to the desirable isothiocyanate and indole products; for instance, microwave cooking or rapid boiling have been shown to completely destroy myrosinase activity. It is also important to note that because glucosinolates are water soluble, they

can leach into cooking water and are lost if it is discarded.

Some gut bacteria are known to produce myrosinase, allowing glucosinolates to be converted to isothiocyanates when cruciferous vegetables are digested. Some people's gut bacteria are more efficient at doing this than others, allowing them to derive more benefit from cooked cruciferous vegetables. In situations where gut bacteria are being reduced or eliminated, for instance during prolonged antibiotic intake, the health benefits from cruciferous vegetables will be much reduced. On top of that, some people are more genetically predisposed than others to benefit from eating cruciferous vegetables: these individuals cannot produce one or more of the enzymes that break down isothiocyanates so they eliminate them more slowly and are therefore exposed to their beneficial effects for a longer time.

### Evidence from human studies

Cruciferous vegetables contain a number of different glucosinolates at varying concentrations. Those that have been identified as potentially beneficial can be found in broccoli, Brussels sprouts, cabbage, cauliflower, kale, watercress and rocket. Furthermore, it appears that sprouts from broccoli seed contain the beneficial compounds in greater concentration than in the fully grown broccoli plant itself.

A recently published study of fruit and vegetable intake found a strong association between consumption of cruciferous vegetables and reductions in prostate-cancer risk. The study population, a group of more than 29,000 predominantly white males, had a 40 per cent decrease in risk of extraprostatic cancer, (defined as stage III or IV), if they were in the group that consumed the most cruciferous vegetables compared to those who consumed the least. The highest-intake group consumed on average 1.1 servings of cruciferous vegetables per day, while the lowest-intake group only consumed an average of 0.1 servings per day. These servings were defined as one US cup of leafy vegetables or one-half US cup of other vegetables such as broccoli and cauliflower. Furthermore, when the vegetables were considered individually, those who ate broccoli or cauliflower more than once a week had a 45 per cent (broccoli) or 52 per cent (cauliflower) lower risk of extraprostatic cancer and a 24 per cent (broccoli) reduction in risk for aggressive prostate cancer, defined as stage III or IV, or Gleason score (see Glossary) greater or equal to 7, than those who ate them less than once per month.

Despite the impressive findings of a number of studies, much of the evidence has been inconsistent. This may be partly due to the problems associated with the assessment of dietary intake of cruciferous vegetables, such as the limitation of accuracy associated with recalling past intake of foods. Furthermore, as previously mentioned, the glucosinolate content of cruciferous vegetables can vary in both type and concentration, can be lost during cooking, and can have a more pronounced effect on certain individuals.

### How do cruciferous vegetables work?

Isothiocyanates and indoles probably act by a number of mechanisms in the prevention and inhibition of prostate cancer. Some of the actions appear to be unique to specific compounds, while others are common to more than one compound. Effects include reduced growth and increased death of cancer cells, lower activation of androgen receptors, less invasion of cancer cells into surrounding tissues, reduced inflammation and the detoxification and removal of cancer-causing compounds.

### What amount of cruciferous vegetables do we eat?

The International Agency for Research on Cancer reported in 2004 that cruciferous vegetables such as cabbage, broccoli, cauliflower, Brussels sprouts and watercress appeared to account for 10–15 per cent of total vegetable intake. Consumption varied across Europe with intakes of around 30g per day in some northern European countries and less than 15g per day in the south. The average intake in North America was reported to be 25–30g per day, with the highest consumption – more than 100g per day – in China.

### Other benefits and risks of eating cruciferous vegetables

Some studies have shown that cruciferous vegetables can lower the risk of coronary heart disease and stroke and reduce inflammation, a factor in many diseases.

Certain cruciferous vegetables, notably broccoli, have a high content of vitamin K which has a role in blood coagulation. Interactions have been seen with warfarin medication but only at intakes much higher than our recommendations. As a note of caution however, cruciferous vegetables can interfere with the uptake of the mineral iodine by the thyroid gland, resulting in growth of the thyroid. Reassuringly, however, a clinical study found no adverse effects. Nonetheless, it would be prudent to ensure an adequate supply of iodine in the diet to avoid straining the thyroid. The richest sources of dietary iodine are seafood and fish but we would also recommend the use of iodised salt in place of regular salt.

## Recommendations

There are no specific guidelines for the consumption of cruciferous vegetables apart from the general guidelines for fruit and vegetable consumption. Research suggests that the risk of prostate cancer is reduced with regular consumption of cruciferous vegetables. It may therefore be beneficial to choose one of the cruciferous vegetables, particularly broccoli, Brussels sprouts, cabbage, cauliflower, kale, watercress or rocket, as one of your daily servings of vegetables or to include them at least several times per week. You may be able to find broccoli sprouts (or sprout the seeds yourself at home) to add to salads, sandwiches or stir-fries. It is also important to remember that to retain as many of the beneficial compounds as possible, cruciferous vegetables should be eaten raw (e.g. coleslaw), or only lightly cooked using cooking methods that use less water, such as steaming.

The summary table to the right details the quantities of cruciferous vegetables consumed in studies where beneficial effects have been noted, as well as our suggested target intake and our definition of a 'good source of' and 'source of' as used for recipes in the book.

| Cruciferous Vegetables | |
|---|---|
| **Effects seen at...** (according to human studies) | More than 3 servings of cruciferous vegetables per week up to 1 serving of cruciferous vegetables per day *or* 2 servings per week of broccoli or cauliflower |
| **Target intake...** | 3–5 80g servings of cruciferous vegetables per week |
| **Good source of...** | 80g |
| **Source of...** | 20g |

# fish

The oils present in cold-water fish belong to a group of fats known as omega-3 fatty acids. Although omega-3 fatty acids are also found in plants and plant foods (notably in flaxseed/rapeseed, canola and walnut), they are the short-chain form which is not easily usable by the body. By contrast, oily fish contain pre-formed long-chain omega-3 fatty acids. These fats are essential for human health with known roles in vision, the immune system and brain function, and they appear to protect against sudden cardiac death. Rates of prostate cancer are low in parts of the world, such as Asia, where oily fish consumption is high leading to the suggestion that fish or fish oils may have protective effects against the disease.

## Evidence from human studies

Though studies in animals and experiments in laboratories show that fish oils have the potential to reduce the risk of development of prostate cancer and to slow its growth, results of human studies are not so clear. Some 15 human epidemiologic studies (studies that examine how various factors affect the occurrence of diseases in population groups) have failed to find a link between the consumption of fish or long-chain omega-3 fatty acids and the occurrence of prostate cancer. The three notable exceptions include a Swedish study that followed up 6,272

men for 30 years and found that men who ate no fish were two to three times more likely to develop prostate cancer than those who ate moderate or high amounts. More encouragingly, there is considerably stronger evidence, of which we give two examples below, that fish intake can reduce the progression of prostate cancer, resulting in lower rates of locally advanced disease, metastatic disease and death.

Among 47,882 men participating in the US Health Professionals Follow-up

Study who were followed up for 12 years, 2,482 cases of prostate cancer were diagnosed, 617 of which were advanced prostate cancer, including 278 metastatic prostate cancers. Eating fish more than three times per week, compared with less than twice per month, was associated with a reduced risk of prostate cancer, with the strongest association being for metastatic cancer where the risk was reduced by 44 per cent. Dark-meat fish had the strongest protective effect, while each additional daily intake of 0.5g of sea-food fatty acid was associated with a 24 per cent decreased risk of metastatic cancer. Another large study found similar protective effects. The US Physicians' Health Study recruited 20,167 men and followed them up for 19 years during which time 2,161 cases of prostate cancer developed. Men who consumed fish five times per week or more had a 48 per cent lower risk of death from prostate cancer than men who consumed fish less than once per week.

These are not the only studies showing that diet after diagnosis may influence the clinical course of prostate cancer. While there is little evidence for an effect of fish or fish fatty acids on the risk of developing prostate cancer, there is a fairly clear indication that fish may offer some protection against disease progression and death from prostate cancer.

### How does fish have its effect?

Numerous laboratory and animal studies have consistently shown that fish oils (or long-chain omega-3 fatty acids) can slow the growth of tumours, prevent their spread and extend life span. Likely mechanisms include the ability of long-chain omega-3 fatty acids from fish to compete with long-chain omega-6 fatty acids (mainly from meat and eggs) for the enzymes that would otherwise convert the omega-6 fatty acids into pro-cancerous products. Increasing the ratio of omega-3 to omega-6 fatty acids in the diet decreased the number of prostate cancer cells in mice, resulting in

longer PSA doubling time. A further important property of fish fatty acids is their ability to prevent the stimulation of growth of prostate-cancer cells by androgens.

Apart from the omega-3 fatty acids, other components of fish, or perhaps the combination, may also be effective against prostate cancer. Seafood is typically high in selenium and oily fish are high in vitamin D, both of which have been linked to protection from prostate cancer.

### How much fish do we eat?

Amounts of fish in the diet vary greatly from one part of the world to another, making important contributions to the diets of some coastal communities, but a lesser contribution in landlocked countries. Fish intake in the UK is low, currently only 51g per week per person; given that the average portion is 140g this is only a third of a portion per week. The most commonly consumed oily fish are salmon, tinned or pickled pilchards, sardines and tuna, canned and smoked mackerel and fresh trout.

### Types of oily fish

Oily fish include kippers, mackerel, pilchards, salmon, trout, herring, sardines, tuna and anchovies in decreasing order of long-chain omega-3 fatty acid content. These fish can be fresh, frozen or tinned, with the exception of tuna which loses the beneficial oils when tinned.

### Other benefits of eating fish

Evidence shows that fish oil can prevent irregular heart rhythm which is probably why it reduces the risk of

sudden cardiac death. It also has an anti-inflammatory effect that may help people suffering from arthritis or other inflammatory conditions. Oily fish may help prevent decline in brain function with age. An additional benefit of fish is that it contains less saturated ('bad') fat than meat. This makes fish a healthier option than meat not only for prostate health, but also for weight management and heart health. Oily fish also contains vitamin D (see vitamin D section) while all fish are a good source of selenium, vitamin B12 and protein.

### Risks of eating oily fish

Pollutants can accumulate in the oils of fish, so no more than four portions of oily fish should be consumed per week. No more than one portion of shark, swordfish or marlin per week should be consumed, as more pollutants accumulate in the oils of

these large predatory fish; pregnant women and children under the age of sixteen should avoid them. These limits do not apply to non-oily fish. In addition, very large amounts of omega-3s can cause bleeding, but this would require more than one portion per day of the average oily fish.

## Recommendations

Given that a protective effect of oily fish is possible, particularly for advanced disease, and that there are other health benefits of eating oily fish, it seems sensible to include it in the diet. In the UK, the recommendations are to consume two portions of fish per week, at least one of which should be oily. This is a minimal, but achievable, amount which may do some good; more would be preferable for optimal effect. Studies have shown benefits at different intakes (see table) but more than two portions per week appear to be required. We recommend two to four portions of oily fish per week, but no more than four because of the pollutants. Other non-oily fish and seafood should also be included in the diet. Note that an average portion is 140g, but can range from about 100–200g.

## Fish

| Effects seen at… (according to human studies) | |
| --- | --- |
| Fish | 2 or more servings per week<br>More than 3 servings per week (metastatic disease)<br>5 or more servings per week (effects on fatal disease)<br>More than 130g per day (possible effects at lower amounts) |
| Fish (mostly oily) | 'A large part of the diet' (effects seen at lower amounts) |
| Fresh or smoked fish | 1 or more servings per week |
| Preserved fish | 1–3 servings per month |
| **Target intake…** | 2–4 portions per week |
| **Good source of…** | 100g |
| **Source of…** | 40g |

# legumes, soya and phytoestrogens

## Legumes

Legumes are plants that produce fruit in the form of pods containing edible seeds; the seeds themselves are also known as legumes or pulses. Examples of legumes are peas, beans, lentils and, surprisingly, peanuts which are often thought of as nuts, although they are in fact legumes. In addition to being excellent sources of protein and fibre, legumes contain many other components that may be beneficial in cancer prevention. Soya beans are among the most commonly consumed legumes, set apart from others by their high content of plant phytochemicals known as phytoestrogens. There is evidence to suggest that both legumes as a whole and soya beans (and soya products) in particular can help fight prostate cancer.

Phytoestrogens are plant compounds that are similar in size and structure to the human hormone oestrogen. The term literally means plant (or phyto) estrogen. Numerous classes of phytoestrogens exist, of which one group in particular, the isoflavones, abundant in soya beans, has been most closely linked to prostate cancer prevention. Although isoflavones are present in many legumes, especially broad beans and peanuts, the richest sources are soya beans and their

products such as tofu and soya milk. Diets in many Asian countries are vegetarian and semi-vegetarian making them rich in plant foods including soya products and therefore phytoestrogens. Given the particularly low rates of prostate cancer in Asian countries, the theory has developed that phytoestrogens are 'phytoprotectants' that protect against prostate cancer.

### Evidence from human studies

Studies have shown a link between high soya and phytoestrogen intake and a reduced risk of prostate cancer. One study attempted to relate the amounts of a number of different foods consumed in 42 countries to the incidence of prostate cancer. Consumption of a large amount of soya products, including soya beans, was associated with a reduced risk of prostate cancer: in fact soya appeared to be four times more effective than any other food studied. Interestingly men who migrate from Japan, where soya intake is particularly high, to the US, have an increased risk of prostate cancer compared to those who stay in Japan, although of course many other factors are likely to be involved as well.

Specific soya foods have been studied in relation to prostate cancer risk. One study investigated the benefit of drinking soya milk: 12,395 men filled out a questionnaire that asked how frequently they used soya milk. Sixteen years later, the number of men who had developed prostate cancer was investigated. Men who drank soya milk once a day appeared to have reduced their risk of prostate cancer by 20 per cent, while those who drank soya milk more than once a day reduced their risk by a massive 70 per cent. Another prospective study investigated 8,173 Japanese men who had moved to Hawaii, using dietary questionnaires. The men were followed up 19 years later to see who had developed prostate cancer. High tofu (a soya product made from soya milk) intake was found to be linked to a reduced risk of developing the disease and the greater the intake, the stronger was the effect. While other studies have also found protective effects from soya products and soya phytoestrogens, not all have shown such a link.

Consumption of non-soya legumes may also reduce prostate cancer risk as shown in the following three studies. The effect of intake of legumes, both including and excluding soya products, was examined in a study in the US and Canada. Men with prostate cancer (1,619) and men without the disease (1,618) were interviewed about their diet. The researchers found that eating 40g of soya foods per day reduced the risk of prostate cancer by 38 per cent,

but eating more than 50g per day of other legumes reduced the risk by 32 per cent. Fourteen thousand men were followed up for six years to examine the effect of diet on prostate cancer risk. The researchers found that eating peas, beans or lentils more than three times per week compared to less than once per month reduced the risk of prostate cancer by 47 per cent. This can be interpreted as a risk reduction of 18–19 per cent with every serving of beans, peas or lentils per week. In the Netherlands Cohort Study 58,279 men gave information on their diet at baseline and those who had developed prostate cancer were identified six years later. Eating 62g of legumes per day appeared to reduce the risk of prostate cancer by 29 per cent. These studies indicate that legumes in general, not just soya beans, have protective effects against prostate cancer, presumably because of other food components than isoflavones. However, just as for soya foods, not all studies show an effect.

Lignans are another class of phytoestrogens that have been linked to a reduced risk of prostate cancer. Lignans are widely available in the diet but are mainly present in fruits, nuts and seeds. They are converted by bacteria in the lower gut to the compounds enterolactone and enterodiol which are then absorbed. Though enterolactone has been shown in laboratory studies to reduce cell division and to kill prostate cancer cells, there is only one study linking a lower risk of prostate cancer with higher blood levels of enterolactone.

Though non-soya legumes appear to reduce risk and lignans may be beneficial, it is soya foods for which there is most evidence of an effect.

## How do these foods and food components work?
The chemical structure of phytoestrogens allows them to act, weakly, like the human hormone, oestrogen, which is essential for both men and women. Isoflavones behave not only as weak oestrogens but also as anti-androgens, opposing the activity of testosterone. As these hormones have roles in the development and progression of prostate cancer, it follows that phytoestrogens may have beneficial effects. Testosterone, and the more potent form of testosterone known as dihydrotestosterone (DHT), cause prostate cancer cells to grow. Oestrogen can suppress testosterone production. Isoflavones and the compounds they are converted to (their metabolites), such as equol, can act like oestrogen to lower testosterone levels resulting in slower tumour growth. Phytoestrogens can also block the conversion of testosterone into the more potent DHT.

The protective effects of soya foods are thought to be due, at least in part, to their isoflavone content. When soya foods are digested, bacteria living in the gut (large intestine) can metabolise one of the isoflavones (daidzein) into an oestrogen-like compound called equol, an antagonist of DHT. Equol can interfere with DHT to reduce its effect and so reduce prostate cancer risk. However, not everyone has intestinal bacteria that can produce equol, so some people may benefit more from soya foods than others. About 60 per cent of vegetarians and 25 per cent of non-vegetarians are equol producers. Gut bacteria can also be affected by use of antibiotics and other dietary factors such as the type of carbohydrate.

Furthermore, some 42 per cent of northern European men are genetically more able (because of a variation in the oestrogen receptor-beta gene) to respond to a high intake of phytoestrogens. A Swedish study showed that these men had an almost 60 per cent lower risk of prostate cancer when they had a high (7.3g per day) rather than low (0.7g per day) intake of phytoestrogen-rich foods (sum of intake of flaxseed, sunflower seeds, berries, peanuts, beans and soya). Interestingly, laboratory studies show that phytoestrogens can also act in ways that are unrelated to hormones and these vary according to the type of phytoestrogen. For example, some are weak antioxidants which can help prevent pre-cancerous damage to cells and genes. In laboratories, scientists have shown that isoflavones can halt the growth and cause the death of prostate cancer cells. They can stop the formation of new blood vessels which are required for tumours to grow and they can help prevent a tumour from spreading (metastatic disease). However, it is likely that these particular effects are too weak to be significant in humans. The way non-soya legumes exert their effects may be through the numerous other components present. These include not only some phytoestrogens, but also fibre and a number of other plant chemicals that

| Legumes | |
| --- | --- |
| **Effects seen at**… | |
| Legumes | At least 4 servings per week *or* 62 g per day to 81g per day |
| Non-soya legumes | 52g per day |
| Beans, lentils, nuts and seeds | More than 31g per day |
| Beans | More than 3 servings per week |
| Baked beans | At least 2 servings per week |
| Garden peas | At least 5 servings per week |
| Peas, beans and lentils | More than 3 servings per week |
| **Target intake**… | 3 to 4 80g servings per week |
| **Good source of**… | 80g |
| **Source of**... | 20g |

## Soya and Soya Products

| Effects seen at... | |
|---|---|
| Soya bean products | More than 2 servings per week, but even better results at more than one per day |
| Soya foods | From 40 to 164g per day |
| Tofu | More than 35g per day *or* More than 5 servings per week *or* 240g per week |
| Soya milk | One serving per day, but better effects seen at more than one serving per day (400ml) |
| **Target intake...** | 3–4 servings of 80g soya food (such as tofu) per week and regular consumption of soya milk |
| **Good source of...** | 80g soya food or 200ml soya milk |
| **Source of...** | 20g soya food or 50ml soya milk |

may work individually, or together, to protect against the disease.

### How much of these foods do we eat?

The amounts of soya foods and legumes in people's diets vary greatly worldwide. In the traditional diets of many countries, legumes are combined with cereals (grains). Legumes are also a great source of fibre. They are a dietary staple in some countries of Asia, Latin America and the Middle East. By contrast, legumes make insignificant contributions to typical North American and most European diets where meat and other animal foods are eaten in higher amounts.

The legumes consumed in the greatest quantities are soya beans and peanuts. Soya bean intake is highest in parts of Asia and higher than average in parts of Africa and Central America. Intake of isoflavones is correspondingly high in Asian countries such as Japan where soya food intake is up to 50 times higher than in the UK. Most of the isoflavones in these diets come from the four major soya products i.e. tofu, miso, natto and soya bean paste.

### Sources

The seeds of leguminous plants (legumes) can be eaten as green vegetables, e.g. broad beans and garden peas, and in some cases they are eaten in their pods as is the case for green beans, runner beans and snow peas (mangetout). Bean sprouts are legumes that have germinated and sprouted. In some cases the seeds can mature and dry on the plant, as in lentils and peanuts. Dietary sources of legumes vary across the world; for example, chilli beans and refried beans are eaten in Mexico, dhal, made from lentils, is eaten in India, pea soup is popular in Sweden and mung bean sprouts are widely consumed in China.

Soya beans, a rich source of isoflavones, are available dried, frozen, roasted (soya nuts) and fresh (edamame beans). Soya beans are very versatile – see the numerous products listed on page 51. Linseed (flaxseed) is the richest source of lignans though rye (rye bran), cashew nuts, cranberries and peanuts also contain lignans. Smaller amounts of several types of phytoestrogens are present in a wide variety of fruits, vegetables, legumes, nuts and seeds, so a variety of such foods may be beneficial.

### Other risks and benefits of eating these foods

There has been some concern about the effect of soya foods on thyroid function as soya can reduce the uptake of iodine by the thyroid (i.e. it behaves as a goitrogen). However, a recent review of the evidence found that there was no need to avoid soya foods provided iodine intake was adequate. Those cutting down on milk and dairy products, which are the major sources of iodine in the UK, to less than 600ml a day, need to ensure a good alternative source of iodine, such as fish. Non-fish eaters would be well advised to take a supplement that contains iodine (usually a multi-vitamin and mineral supplement). Some questions have also been raised about the safety of soya foods on age-related brain diseases such as Alzheimer's disease. These concerns are based

on one human study which suggested a mild detrimental effect on cognitive (learning and memory) function, but the quality of this study has been questioned and the authors themselves acknowledge that it does not prove a link. Other studies have actually shown benefits of soya foods in relation to brain health. The safety of soya foods has been extensively reviewed and their use is approved by the British Dietetic Association and the US Food and Drug Administration.

Phytoestrogens have been associated with many health benefits including reduced risk of other cancers (e.g. breast cancer), reduced cholesterol levels, blood pressure, heart disease and stroke, improved bone health and milder menopausal symptoms in women.

### Recommendations

We recommend the regular consumption of a variety of legumes. Based on the published evidence it appears that 3–4 portions per week may be beneficial (80g being one portion). We also recommend an increased intake of soya phytoestrogens (isoflavones) by including soya beans and soya products in the diet. It is difficult to recommend quantities of specific soya foods because the published studies have looked at a variety of soya-containing foods such as soya milk or tofu. However, the data seem to indicate that, again, 3-4 portions of approximately 80g of soya foods per week could have some benefit. Replacing some cow's milk with soya milk would be a simple way to achieve

this, in addition to consuming other soya products. The effects of soya foods were dose-responsive in some studies, meaning that the more that was eaten, the greater the effect. In practical terms, this means that any intake is better than none, even if you cannot meet the target amounts.

The table lists the amounts of legumes and soya foods found to be beneficial in published studies. Our recommendations are derived from these data and our interpretation of the amount that constitutes a 'good source of' or 'source of' these foods (indicated on the relevant recipes) is shown. It is also advisable to consume a variety of fruits, vegetables, grains, nuts and seeds (particularly linseed and rye) because, although they contain only minimal amounts of phytoestrogens, they will increase overall phytoprotectant intake and form part of a healthy, balanced diet.

**Note: a portion of soya foods can constitute a portion of legumes, but a portion of any other legume cannot be considered as a portion of soya, as it will not contain the isoflavones which may be responsible for the beneficial effect of soya.**

# polyphenols

Thousands of chemicals present in plants are part of a diverse group of plant chemicals known as polyphenols. These give colour, odour and flavour to foods and drinks and have antioxidant and antimicrobial activities which help prevent foods from going off. Many polyphenols are said to have diverse health-protecting qualities and research indicates that they may slow the growth of human cancers, including prostate cancer. Several polyphenol-rich foods are thought to be beneficial in reducing the risk of prostate cancer but the evidence is strongest for green tea, with growing interest in pomegranate. Some polyphenols – the phytoestrogens, as found in soya foods – are discussed in a separate section.

Green tea has been used for centuries to prevent and treat chronic diseases and evidence shows it has protective effects against heart disease. The first recorded incidence of tea drinking dates back to 2737 BC; now it is the most widely consumed drink in the world, second only to water. Numerous polyphenols are present in tea accounting for 30 per cent of the dry weight of the leaves. Green tea leaves can be fermented to become black tea or partially fermented to become oolong tea. Green tea, in particular, has generated interest in prostate-cancer prevention owing to the low incidence of all types of cancer, including prostate cancer, in

Asian populations where green tea is a popular drink. A growing number of studies supports this association.

Pomegranate is the fruit of a deciduous shrub that has been described as nature's power fruit. It originated in the Middle East but is now grown in the Far East, India, the Mediterranean and the Americas. A symbol of fertility, life and healing, the pomegranate has been used for centuries for medicinal purposes and features in the heraldic crests

of several medical institutions including that of the Royal College of Physicians of London. Components of pomegranate are said to have anti-inflammatory, anti-atherogenic (reducing build-up of deposits in arteries) and, more recently, anti-cancer effects.

**Evidence from human studies**
The results of several studies suggest a protective effect of green tea on prostate cancer. In a much-cited case-control study of men in southeast

China, 130 men with prostate cancer and 274 men without it were asked about their tea-drinking habits (mostly green tea). Analysis showed that tea-drinkers had a 72 per cent lower risk of developing the disease than non-tea-drinkers and the risk appeared to be reduced with duration, quantity and frequency of tea consumption. The best effects were seen with tea drinking over 40 years, consumption of more than 1.5 kg of tea leaves yearly and drinking more than 1 litre (3 cups) daily. The effect was dose-responsive, meaning the greater the intake of tea, the greater the benefit; this means that some tea drinking is better than none at all. In a similar study conducted in Canada on 617 men with prostate cancer and 637 men without it, more than 500ml (two cups) of tea daily was linked to a significantly decreased risk of prostate cancer and the effects were again dose-responsive. It should be noted that the tea consumed was not only green tea.

A prospective study carried out in Japan assessed green-tea consumption in nearly 50,000 men at a certain time point. Fourteen to 17 years later, the number of men who had developed prostate cancer was determined: while analysis showed that green tea had no effect on total prostate cancer it did reduce the risk of developing advanced disease (cancer that has spread beyond the prostate). The effect was dose-dependant and the greatest effects were seen with consumption of more than 1.25 litres (five cups) per day which reduced the risk of advanced disease by 47 per cent.

An intervention study was carried out in men at high risk of prostate cancer. Thirty men were given a pill containing green tea polyphenols to take everyday for a year and 30 men were given a dummy pill (a placebo). After a year, 30 per cent of the men in the placebo group (nine men) developed prostate cancer while only 3 per cent (one man) developed the disease in those receiving the green-tea pill. This implies that the green-tea pills prevented, or at least delayed, the onset of prostate cancer.

While there are a number of studies to link green tea with cancer-fighting properties, some studies have indicated that even black tea may be protective. The link, however, has not been proved, the evidence is limited and some studies found that tea consumption had no effect. Research in this area is ongoing.

The effects of pomegranate on prostate cancer have been assessed in laboratory and animal studies. These studies have had promising results showing that pomegranate can reduce cell growth and tumour size. However, to date, only one trial has been carried out in humans. In this study 46 men with rising PSA after surgery or radiotherapy were given a glass (237ml) of pomegranate juice per day. Every three months, blood PSA levels were measured. The rise in PSA was significantly slowed down and in seven subjects, PSA levels even dropped. This may indicate a beneficial effect on cancer progression. Importantly, the juice did not cause any adverse effects. The results are promising but do not prove a link and other studies

are under way to investigate further the potential benefits.

## How do polyphenols work?
The anti-cancer effects of green tea are attributed to the many polyphenols present. The most important of these are known collectively as green tea catechins. The mechanisms by which green tea catechins function are interesting as it would seem they have effects against early prostate cancer which is hormone-dependent and also against hormone-independent disease which occurs at a later stage in disease progression.

Androgens stimulate prostate cells to grow and divide, making androgens a target in disease prevention and treatment. In the laboratory green tea catechins have been found to prevent testosterone from being converted into its more active form 5-alpha-dihydroxytestosterone and so may prevent the growth of androgen-sensitive prostate cancer cells. Animal studies have shown that achievable amounts of green-tea polyphenols in the diet reduced the growth not only of androgen-sensitive cells but also of androgen-insensitive cells. These effects were accompanied by increased survival rates. Evidence shows that green tea can kill prostate cancer cells without affecting healthy cells, delay tumour development, reduce the risk of cancer spread and even prevent the formation of the new blood vessels required for tumours to grow. The evidence implies that green tea has roles at multiple stages of the disease and so can be considered not only as a preventive but as a therapeutic agent. Laboratory and

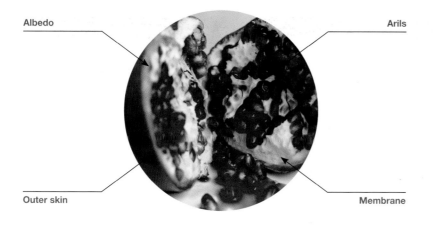

Albedo

Arils

Outer skin

Membrane

animal studies have also shown that green tea may affect the later stages of disease by preventing invasion into surrounding tissues (i.e. metastasis).

Studies carried out in animals have shown that the polyphenols extracted from the juice, peel and oil of pomegranate may have numerous effects on prostate cancer. These include reported abilities to reduce tumour incidence, delay tumour initiation (the time to getting a tumour), cause prostate cancer cells to die, decrease PSA levels and slow tumour growth, thereby increasing survival and improving quality of life.

Although this evidence looks promising, there is less evidence for these mechanisms being relevant in humans. The polyphenols may not be absorbed efficiently into the bloodstream and there are questions surrounding, for example, the quantities required, the type of tea, and the effects in different ethnicities.

Other mechanisms, as explained below, may be more important.

Bacteria in the gut, known as gut microflora, play a hugely important role in the effects of polyphenols in the body. The microflora convert the polyphenols into the form in which they appear in the blood and are delivered to tissues where they can have an effect. For instance, pomegranates contain a class of polyphenols known as ellagitannins and are the only dietary source of galligatannins. These compounds are converted by the gut microflora into urolithins which are probably responsible for the anti-cancer properties ascribed to pomegranates. Due to differences in microflora, some people produce more urolithins than others so some will benefit more than others from eating pomegranates. Interestingly, it is not only pomegranates that contain ellagitanins; walnuts, berries, particularly raspberries and, to a lesser extent, strawberries, also contain

ellagitanins in smaller amounts and these too are converted to urolithins. It follows that raspberries may also be protective though they have not been studied specifically.

### What quantities of polyphenols do we consume?

Two and a half million metric tonnes of dried tea are manufactured annually and consumption varies greatly worldwide. Twenty per cent of tea produced is green tea and this is consumed in the highest amounts in Asian countries and a few countries in North Africa and the Middle East. Black tea makes up 78 per cent of total tea and is popular in the West and in some Asian countries; the remaining 2 per cent is oolong tea, produced and consumed in southeastern China. Tea consumption varies hugely between individuals ranging from no tea to 20 cups per day.

Pomegranate consumption also varies world-wide with production mainly in the Mediterranean and Afghanistan, India, China, Japan, Russia and some parts of the US. Although the fruit is produced seasonally – typically from September to January in the Northern Hemisphere – the juice is available all year round.

### Sources
Polyphenols are widespread in fruits, vegetables and drinks but those that have been shown to be particularly relevant to prostate cancer are green tea, pomegranate and possibly raspberries. Green tea needs to be brewed for five minutes to allow enough time for the active components to be released into the

water in sufficient quantities. Black tea, which is made by fermenting green tea leaves, also contains polyphenols and may be benefical in prostate cancer, though the evidence here is weak.

Polyphenols exist in various parts of pomegranate fruit and many exist in the peel. Drinking pomegranate juice may be more beneficial than eating the arils (the seeds surrounded by the little sacs of liquid) as the juice usually includes the peel extract. Pomegranate can be reduced to a syrup, also known as pomegranate paste or molasses. This product is used in Middle Eastern cooking and can be bought in specialist Iranian shops: it can be made at home by reducing the juice in a pan with a little lemon juice and sugar. As noted, ellagitannin polyphenols are also contained in berries, particularly raspberries, although the quantities are not as high as in pomegranate.

There is speculation that a number of other polyphenols have anti-prostate-cancer properties. These include resveratrol in red wine and red grape juice and curcumin in turmeric, ginger and cardamom. The research in these areas is in its infancy and so we will have to wait to see whether or not these foods have a noticeable effect.

### Other risks and benefits associated with polyphenols

It has been suggested that green tea consumption may benefit many chronic health problems such as inflammatory conditions, diabetes, obesity, cancer and cardiovascular disease, the latter because of beneficial effects on blood cholesterol.

| Green tea | |
|---|---|
| **Effects seen at...** | |
| tea (all types) | More than 500ml per day (2 cups) but less also has an effect |
| tea (mostly green) | Greater than 3 cups per day (1 litre) |
| green tea | More than 5 cups per day but less also has an effect |
| **Target intake...** | 4–6 cups per day |
| **Good source of...** | 1 cup |

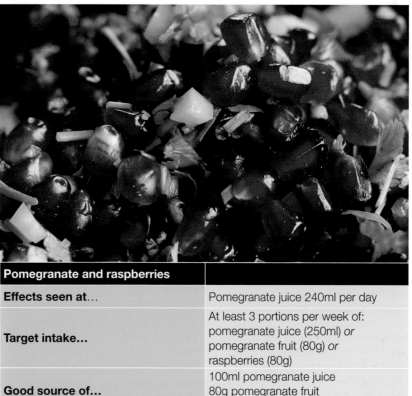

| Pomegranate and raspberries | |
|---|---|
| **Effects seen at...** | Pomegranate juice 240ml per day |
| **Target intake...** | At least 3 portions per week of: pomegranate juice (250ml) *or* pomegranate fruit (80g) *or* raspberries (80g) |
| **Good source of...** | 100ml pomegranate juice 80g pomegranate fruit 80g raspberries |
| **Source of...** | 25ml juice 20ml pomegranate fruit 20g raspberries |

Polyphenols may also improve immune function and have been shown to reduce lower urinary tract symptoms and improve quality of life in men with benign prostate enlargement. An additional benefit of consumption of green tea rather than black tea is that milk and sugar are generally not added.

Fruits such as pomegranate and berries which contain helpful polyphenols are in any case beneficial as part of a healthy, balanced diet in addition to their possible effects on prostate cancer. Pomegranate consumption has been linked not only with reduced risk of prostate cancer but with beneficial effects on the risk of cardiovascular disease.

It is widely accepted that polyphenol-rich foods such as green tea and pomegranate are non-toxic and safe to consume. While green tea is considered safe, the possibility of harmful effects of excessive tea consumption or drinking very hot beverages cannot be ruled out. These risks can be removed by limiting tea intake to no more that six cups per day; this amount has been shown to be beneficial with benefits also observed at lower levels. This is a conservative limit as intakes in Asia far exceed this amount. Tea could also be left to cool slightly before consumption. The caffeine in green tea may irritate the stomach, cause insomnia or rapid heartbeat, but decaffeinated green tea is available.

There is no evidence of toxicity from pomegranate in humans, even in North Africa where intakes are the highest

in the world. Although pomegranate has a long history of use as a food in many cultures and no studies using pomegranate have found any adverse effects, some people may be allergic to the seeds, so those with known fruit or nut allergies should look out for signs and symptoms of allergic reactions.

## Recommendations

As effects of green tea have been seen at quantities of six cups per day, we recommend consumption of four to six cups of green tea per day. This is a safe amount to consume. Effects have been seen at lower doses so any amount would be better than none even if you cannot reach the ideal six cups. Men taking medication for prostate cancer should not consume more than three cups per day without consulting their physician, as it may potentially slow the rate of drug clearance.

The quantities of polyphenol sources that were effective in studies are shown in the tables on page 29, as well as in our definition of what constitutes a 'source' or 'good source' in a recipe. In the case of pomegranate and raspberries, it is difficult to recommend a particular amount because only one study of pomegranate has been conducted in humans and no data exist for raspberries. It is likely that long-term regular consumption of pomegranate and raspberries, i.e. roughly three portions per week, would be required for possible benefits.

# tomatoes and lycopene

Lycopene is a natural carotenoid pigment that is responsible for the red colour of some fruits and vegetables, notably tomatoes. Carotenoids cannot be made in the body and so must be obtained from the diet. In the body, some carotenoids can be converted into vitamin A, while others, including lycopene, act as antioxidants. As lycopene is primarily found in tomatoes, it is this source that is most often studied. However, tomatoes are also an excellent source of other nutrients, including folate, vitamins A, C and E, potassium and various other carotenoids and phytochemicals, such as polyphenols, some of which may also be associated with lower cancer risk. It is therefore possible that the anti-cancer effects seen with tomatoes are not due to lycopene alone.

The absorption of lycopene (and other carotenoids) from foods such as tomatoes is helped both by heating and by food-processing which help release the lycopene from plant tissues. The addition of a small amount of fat (e.g. olive oil as found in a tomato-based pasta sauce) in which carotenoids are soluble also helps their absorption. Lycopene from fresh watermelon appears to be absorbed well without requiring heating or processing.

Twelve small clinical trials have investigated the potential impact of lycopene or tomato consumption on prostate cancer risk or spread. These have mostly been in prostate cancer patients scheduled for prostate removal. Almost all of these trials have found evidence of a good effect on PSA, a marker used for prostate cancer diagnosis and progression (e.g. decreased concentration, decreased velocity, increased stabilisation). In one such study in the US, 32 men with localised prostate cancer (awaiting prostate removal) recorded a 20 per cent fall in PSA and a 21 per cent decrease in DNA damage after three weeks of consuming a daily meal of pasta with tomato sauce containing 30mg of lycopene (approximately ½kg tomatoes). When compared to a similar but smaller group of prostate cancer patients that had not received the tomato sauce meal, those eating the tomato sauce had 28 per cent less damage to their prostate DNA. The amount of lycopene found in the patients' blood had doubled after the three weeks of supplementation while that in the prostate tissue had trebled.

Population studies have suggested ideal levels of lycopene intake ranging from 5–35mg per day. However it seems that blood levels can be maximised at an intake of 5–10mg lycopene per day. The number of tomato servings shown to have a good effect on prostate cancer risk also varies from as little as three servings per week to over nine, with an effect for cooked tomato sauce being seen at two or more servings per week.

### Evidence from human studies

According to a number of population studies, men who have a greater dietary intake of either lycopene-containing foods or tomatoes appear to have a lower risk of developing prostate cancer. When results of 21 such studies were combined, researchers concluded that although tomato products may help prevent prostate cancer, the effect is modest and restricted to those eating large quantities. For instance, men who ate cooked tomatoes or tomato products frequently had a 19 per cent reduced risk of getting prostate cancer when compared to those who did not.

In a study of more than 48,000 American health professionals, those who ate two or more portions a week of cooked tomato sauce were 23 per cent less likely to develop prostate cancer than those who consumed tomato sauce less than once a month. The same study also reported a decrease in prostate cancer risk, though smaller, for the men with higher intakes of lycopene-containing foods in general.

While these results are encouraging, not all such studies have found an effect on prostate cancer risk with tomato or lycopene consumption. This may be partly due to the known difficulties in measuring food intake accurately, particularly where intakes of lycopene are low. A 2007 US Food and Drug Administration review concluded that currently there was no credible evidence to support a qualified health claim for lycopene, though there was very limited credible evidence for a qualified health claim for tomatoes and/or tomato sauce and a reduced risk of prostate cancer.

### How does lycopene work?

Lycopene is the principal carotenoid present in tomatoes although they also contain significant amounts of two other carotenoids. While lycopene is a highly potent antioxidant, there is limited support for this being its major function in reducing prostate cancer risk. In

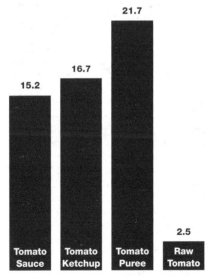

**Lycopene content in mg per 100g of food**

fact, tissue levels of lycopene appear to be too low for it to play a meaningful antioxidant role. The prostate has levels of the antioxidant alpha-tocopherol (vitamin E) that are 162 times as high as those of lycopene. It now appears more likely that bioactive oxidation products of lycopene, the lycopenoids, are responsible for some of its anti-cancer activity and for the beneficial effects of tomato product consumption. Mechanisms for which there is greater support include induction of death of cancer cells, reduction of damage to DNA, and decreasing androgen levels or activity; for instance, serum testosterone concentrations were significantly decreased in rats that were fed lycopene for four days. It is important to be aware that whole food sources such as tomatoes appear to be more effective than lycopene alone, probably because of the synergism between a number of active food components.

### How much lycopene are we getting?

According to the most recent UK National Diet and Nutrition Survey, 67 per cent of men between the ages of 19 and 64 consumed raw tomatoes and only 26 per cent consumed cooked tomatoes, during the week of the survey. Of those who ate raw tomatoes, the average intake was equivalent to about two tomatoes per week. Of those who ate cooked tomatoes the average intake was equivalent to only a third of a tin of tomatoes per week. There are of course other sources of lycopene in the diet that were not taken into account, such as pizza and ketchup.

Other figures on men's tomato consumption come from the EPIC

(European Prospective Investigation into Cancer and Nutrition) study and show that the intake of tomatoes and tomato products varies widely across Europe, ranging from 15g per day in the Netherlands to 163g per day in Greece, with an average intake of 64g per day. The average consumption of tomatoes in the US rose considerably at the beginning of the 1990s and levelled off to around 22g per day for fresh tomatoes (less than two medium-sized tomatoes per week) in 2000. However, the consumption of processed tomato products is much greater in the US and provides the greatest contribution to lycopene intake in the diet there.

### Sources of lycopene in the diet

At least 85 per cent of the lycopene in our diet comes from tomatoes and tomato products though it is also found in watermelon, pink grapefruit, guava and rosehip. The lycopene content of tomatoes is variable and increases with ripening, with very red plum tomatoes providing the most. The best sources of lycopene are sun-dried tomatoes, tomato paste, purée and ketchup, as the tomatoes have been concentrated which gives more lycopene per gram of food. An ideal way of increasing lycopene in your diet is to add an extra tablespoon or two of one of these products to tomato-based dishes that you already cook. These condensed sources, along with tinned tomatoes, are a better source of lycopene than raw tomatoes. The chart on the left illustrates the differences in the lycopene content of processed tomato products and raw tomatoes. The table on page 48 details other dietary sources of lycopene.

### Other benefits and risks of lycopene

Lycopene may have additional benefits as it has been shown to reduce plasma LDL ('bad') cholesterol and to help to reduce the risk of heart attacks, improve immune function and reduce inflammation. Although lycopene is available in supplement form, those undergoing chemotherapy or radiotherapy should be cautious in taking it in that form as the effect of taking antioxidant supplements during chemotherapy or radiotherapy is unclear. However, the consumption of fruits and vegetables high in antioxidants is believed to be safe during cancer treatment.

### Recommendations

As the level of lycopene in the blood (and tissues) reflects dietary intake, foods containing lycopene, particularly tomatoes and tomato products, need to be consumed regularly (strictly speaking, daily, because of rate of clearance of lycopene) to ensure a continuous supply. We recommend eating meals with a tomato-based sauce at least twice per week. Sources of lycopene other than tomatoes, such as watermelon, have also been used in the recipes to encourage its intake.

The summary table to the right details the quantities of tomatoes consumed in some studies where beneficial effects have been noted, as well as our suggested target intake and our definition of a 'good source of' and 'a source of' lycopene in the recipes.

| Lycopene | |
|---|---|
| **Effects seen at...**<br>(according to the study) | 3 servings per week to more than 9 servings per week of tomatoes *or* 2 or more servings of cooked tomatoes per week |
| **Target intake...** | 2 or more servings of cooked tomatoes per week |
| **Good source of...** | 5mg lycopene |
| **Source of...** | 1mg lycopene |

# selenium

Selenium is a trace mineral essential for human health which takes its name from Selene, the Greek goddess of the moon. A number of enzymes that carry out vital functions in the body – including important antioxidant enzymes – rely on selenium for their activity. Lower selenium intakes or levels in body tissues have been linked to higher death rates, greater cancer risk, poor immune function, a reduced ability to deal with viral infections, lower fertility and age-related brain decline. Research suggests that not only may a higher selenium intake reduce the risk of prostate cancer but, perhaps more importantly, it may be able to suppress the spread of cancer outside the prostate. Many studies have shown that the effect of selenium is even greater in smokers.

## Evidence from human trials

The Nutritional Prevention of Cancer (NPC) trial carried out in the Eastern United States provided compelling evidence that selenium could reduce both the risk of developing cancer and the risk of dying from it. A group of 1,312 elderly volunteers, mostly men, were randomly assigned to take either a 200 mcg supplement of selenium yeast or a placebo yeast (dummy tablet) each day for an average period of 4½ years. At the end of 6½ years, the treatment was assessed. In the group that had received selenium rather than the placebo, 37 per cent fewer cases of cancer developed

and 50 per cent fewer people died of cancer. Most remarkable of all, there were 63 per cent fewer cases of prostate cancer. In a follow-up two years later, the effect was slightly less impressive but there were still 49 per cent fewer cases of prostate cancer in those that had received selenium.

However, when the differing rates of prostate biopsy in the selenium and placebo groups were taken into account, it appeared that the only men to benefit from selenium

supplementation were those whose PSA was less than 4 when they entered the trial and whose blood selenium was relatively low (i.e. plasma selenium less than 106ng/ml).

A further and much larger American trial – SELECT – did not find any benefit of the same dose of selenium on prostate cancer risk, though a different form of selenium was used. More importantly, SELECT men already had quite high blood levels of selenium (average plasma selenium 135ng/ml) before they joined the trial and, based on the earlier NPC trial results, it could have been predicted that no benefit of giving extra selenium to such men would have been seen.

However, from NPC trial evidence, it would seem that European men, whose blood levels of selenium (average plasma selenium 71ng/ml) are considerably lower than those in the US, could well benefit from increasing their selenium intake. We also now know that because of their genetic make-up, some men need more selenium than others for protection from prostate cancer.

### How does selenium work?

The remarkable results of the NPC trial encouraged much research to understand how selenium was having its effect. In fact there is evidence that selenium can act through all the mechanisms shown on pages 9–10. Different mechanisms are likely to come into play at different stages of the disease and according to the type of cancer. Many of the effects of selenium occur through selenoproteins, some of which act as enzymes; amounts in the diet need to be high enough to make these selenoproteins. Selenium is transported to body tissues by selenoprotein P, which needs a higher selenium intake to optimise it than is usually consumed in Europe. Furthermore, the amount of a specific form of selenium – not a selenoprotein – that has powerful anti-cancer effects appears to increase as intake goes up. As mentioned above, some people are genetically less able to make the protective selenoproteins, but a higher

dietary intake may help to compensate in such people. In the future it will be possible to tell who is more or less predisposed by a simple genetic test.

### How much selenium are we getting?

Selenium enters the food chain through plants and the amount present in crops varies according to local conditions. Of particular importance is the underlying geology because it determines the amount and type of selenium present and the nature of the soil because this affects take-up by the plant.

Because of these factors, intake of selenium varies widely from one part of the world to another as shown in the figure below. In an enormous country like China, it can be both very high in some areas and very low in others. In North America and particularly Canada, intake levels are generally good but in European countries, particularly those of Eastern Europe, intakes are much lower and may be insufficient for the body's requirements.

The amount of selenium in the UK diet and that of many other European countries has declined considerably in recent decades. This is largely due to the fall in imports of selenium-rich strong wheat flour from Canada which we used to import for bread

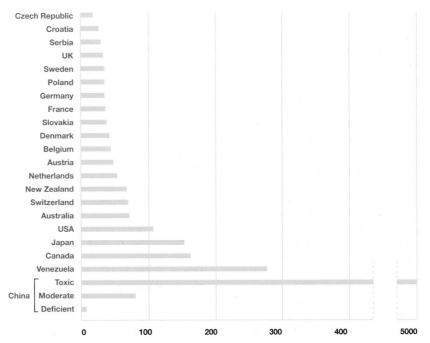

**Selenium intake levels (mcg/d) in different countries**

making. Other factors have also contributed such as breeding cereals for increased grain yield, the fall in acid rain that deposited selenium (along with sulphur) and the increased use of sulphur in fertilizers which competes with selenium for uptake into the plant. In the UK for instance, current selenium intake is only about 60 per cent of what it was 30 years ago and does not now meet government recommended levels.

### Sources of selenium in the diet
Brazil nuts are the richest natural source of selenium but their selenium content is very variable, ranging from 0.03 to 512mg/g fresh weight. Nuts bought with their shells on appear to contain more selenium than ready-shelled nuts. Brazil nuts also contain a chemical element called barium and a radioactive element known as radium. Using Brazil nuts as your sole source of selenium is not advisable, as toxic levels of these chemicals could be reached. Offal, e.g. liver and particularly kidney, are the next best sources of selenium, followed by fish and seafood. In the UK diet, meat and poultry make the biggest contribution to selenium intake. Game, if eaten, is quite a good source. In countries with high or relatively high selenium intakes (e.g. North America) there will be good levels of selenium in wheat, bread or other cereals which will therefore make a substantial contribution, but wheat and cereals are not very good sources in most of Europe.

### Risk of excessive selenium intake
Selenium, though essential, is toxic in high amounts. The UK Department of Health has set a fairly conservative upper limit of 450mcg per day.

### Recommendations
We recommend a target overall consumption of 100–150mcg per day which should be sufficient to raise the concentration in your blood (and prostate) to levels associated with protective effects. Smokers may wish to aim for the higher end of the range. Good dietary sources of selenium and their selenium content (in mcg/g) are listed on page 48. In the recipes, we have considered 40mcg or more per serving to be a 'good source' of selenium and 10–39 mcg per serving to be a 'source' of selenium.

Refer to the figure on page 35 to see the level of selenium intake you may already be getting from the typical diet in your country. If the background intake is low, and you do not think you can increase your intake sufficiently from your diet, you may decide to supplement. However, we suggest you supplement with no more than 100mcg per day, preferably as selenium yeast. Remember that your total intake from all sources should *never* exceed 450mcg per day.

# vitamin D

Vitamin D is more than just a vitamin, it is also converted to a hormone in the body. It enters the body as the inactive compounds vitamin D3 (cholecalciferol) and vitamin D2 (ergocalciferol) and is converted into the active form $1,25(OH)_2D3$ (calcitriol), as shown in the figure on page 37. The main source of vitamin D3 comes from the action of sunlight on a cholesterol compound in the skin, but it can also be obtained by eating some animal foods such as fish, eggs and plant foods such as sun-dried shiitake mushrooms. These non-active forms of vitamin D undergo two processes in the body to produce the active form. The first process takes place in the liver where 25(OH)D (calcidiol) is produced. This then circulates in the blood to the kidneys and other tissues where it is converted into the active form, $1,25(OH)_2D$. Blood levels of 25(OH)D can show whether vitamin D status is adequate.

Factors that affect the level of vitamin D in our bodies include lack of exposure to sufficient sunlight, inadequate intake from diet and other factors including obesity (vitamin D hides in fat), medication, sunscreen use, skin covered with clothing, skin pigmentation and age. A 70-year-old produces approximately four times less vitamin D in the skin than a 20-year-old.

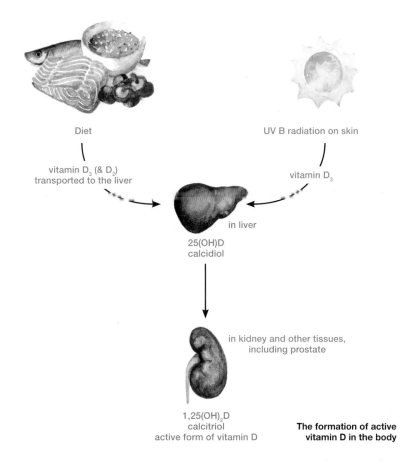

Diet

UV B radiation on skin

vitamin D$_3$ (& D$_2$)
transported to the liver

vitamin D$_3$

in liver

25(OH)D
calcidiol

in kidney and other tissues,
including prostate

1,25(OH)$_2$D
calcitriol
active form of vitamin D

**The formation of active
vitamin D in the body**

The best-known function of vitamin D is to help us absorb calcium from the diet to build healthy bones. However we now know that receptors for vitamin D, through which vitamin D interacts, are present in most cells of the body suggesting that vitamin D has other functions.

### Evidence from human studies

The 'vitamin D-cancer hypothesis' was born when it was observed that people with a history of exposure to high levels of sunlight had a lower risk of a number of cancers. For instance, a significant north–south trend in prostate cancer mortality was found in a 1992 US study, with higher rates in the north where UV radiation was lower. Furthermore, blacks have levels of 25(OH)D that are approximately half those of whites and a 60 per cent greater risk of prostate cancer.

However, studies based on blood levels of 25(OH)D or vitamin-D intake do not generally support a link between vitamin D and prostate cancer. The two studies that suggested an increased risk when levels of 25(OH)D were low were conducted in Nordic countries where vitamin D levels get very low in the winter months. In one such study investigating 19,000 Finnish men, those with 25(OH)D levels in the bottom half of the range (below 40 nmol/L) were found to have a 70 per cent higher risk of developing prostate cancer than those with levels in the top half. For younger men with 25(OH)D levels in the bottom half, incidence of prostate cancer was 3.5 times higher than for those with levels in the top half, and their incidence of invasive cancer was 6.3 times higher. However, a later study in Nordic populations, while also finding an increased risk at low 25(OH)D levels, found an increased risk in men with the highest values (above 80 nmol/L), suggesting that both low and high vitamin D status could increase risk.

Another strand of evidence for a link between vitamin D and prostate cancer is the fact that men with a particular feature in the DNA that codes for their vitamin D receptor – 14 per cent of men of European descent – are more susceptible to this cancer when their blood levels of 25(OH)D are low, and these men also have an increased risk of more aggressive cancer.

As far as we know, there is only one trial of vitamin D in men with prostate cancer: a small Canadian study reported encouraging results in a group of 15 men with recurrent prostate cancer from a daily dose of 50mcg (2000 IU) vitamin D3. PSA levels dropped or stabilised in nine of the men for as long as 21 months and PSA doubling time increased in 14 men, indicating a reduction in the rate at which PSA levels were increasing.

Taken overall, the evidence for an effect of vitamin D on the risk of developing prostate cancer is confusing. However, the apparent increased risk at high vitamin D levels might be explained by other factors that could muddy the results. For instance, a high intake of milk, if fortified, will increase vitamin D intake but will also increase calcium intake which can increase the risk of prostate cancer. Vitamin D intake is also associated with vitamin A intake (another fat-soluble vitamin) which may also have antagonistic effects. Another factor that is difficult to account for is obesity which lowers both vitamin D status and PSA.

### How does vitamin D work?

$1,25(OH)_2D$ has a number of anti-cancer properties: it causes the death of cancer cells and helps control the process by which they invade surrounding tissue. Directly or indirectly, $1,25(OH)_2D$ controls more than 200 genes, including those responsible for the regulation of cell division, cell death and the creation of new blood vessels without which a cancer cannot grow.

Many cells, including prostate cells, contain the enzyme that is responsible for the conversion of $25(OH)D$ to $1,25(OH)_2D$ so they can produce active vitamin D independently of the kidneys. Low levels of circulating $1,25(OH)_2D$ have been associated with an increased risk of aggressive disease. Unfortunately, when prostate cells become cancerous, they appear to lose the ability to produce $1,25(OH)_2D$. For that reason, the important time to have good vitamin D status may be many years before the cancer develops.

### How much vitamin D are we getting?

Most of the vitamin D (90 per cent) in our bodies is made in the skin following exposure to sunlight. Above (or below) latitude 37°, from November to February there is insufficient sunlight of the right wavelength to produce vitamin D. The time of day is also important; for instance in the UK, at 54° of latitude, the appropriate wavelength of sunlight is only available between 11am and 3pm from March through to October. Cloud cover also inhibits vitamin D production, as does pollution, sunscreen, enveloping clothing, elderly and dark skin. People with dark skins produce no more than 5–19 per cent of the vitamin D produced in light-skinned people. Intake from diet is therefore much more important in such people and at northern latitudes, particularly in the winter.

The level of $25(OH)D$ measured in blood serum shows the extent of deficiency. Many scientists think the level should be approximately 75nmol/L (30ng/ml) to provide optimal health protection. However, with the exception of Norway, where vitamin D-rich oily fish consumption is relatively high, vitamin D status in Europe in winter does not reach such levels. A recent investigation showed that low vitamin D status was widespread in white British adults aged 45 with 87 per cent having levels of $25(OH)D$ during the winter/spring below the 75nmol/L thought to be required for optimal bone health, and 47 per cent having levels low enough to warrant vitamin D supplementation. A UK study of over-65-year-olds showed that 8 per cent had blood concentrations of $25(OH)D$ lower than the minimum 25nmol/L needed to prevent rickets and softening of the bones, while 97 per cent were not consuming the minimum recommended level of 10mog/d vitamin D from food. Intakes in Germany and the Netherlands are almost as low though slightly higher in Finland where more oily fish is consumed.

### Current guidelines on vitamin D intake

For UK adults under the age of 65 years, there is no recommended intake level for vitamin D. For those over this age or at risk of deficiency, the suggested intake is 10mcg per day. However this level is set to prevent the onset of osteomalacia (softening of the bones), and does not take account of the additional roles of vitamin D. The adequate intakes suggested in the US are 5mcg per day for adults aged 19–50, 10mcg for adults aged 51–70 years, and 15mcg for those over 70. However, many scientists believe these guidelines to be too low.

### Food sources of vitamin D

Very few foods naturally contain vitamin D. Oily fish are the best sources. Fortified cereals, margarine and most reduced- or low-fat spreads are also an important source due to the regularity with which they are consumed. Foods such as milk and orange juice are fortified in some countries (e.g. in the US), resulting in a higher vitamin D intake there. The table on page 48 shows food sources of vitamin D.

### Risk of excessive vitamin D intake

Excessive intake of vitamin D can promote excessive levels of calcium in blood. However, vitamin D doses up to 25mcg (1000 IU) per day appear to have no associated toxicity and this is the safe upper level that has been set by the UK Expert Group on Vitamins and Minerals for supplementary vitamin D intake. The EU Scientific Committee on Food Opinion and the US Standing Committee on the Scientific Evaluation of Dietary Reference Intakes have set a higher safe intake, 50mcg (2000 IU) per day. However, remember as discussed above, that some studies have found an increased risk of prostate cancer, particularly of aggressive prostate cancer, in men with higher vitamin D status.

### Other benefits of vitamin D

In addition to its classical function in bone health, there is good evidence for a benefit of vitamin D in prevention of colorectal cancer. Furthermore, combined results from 18 trials showed that vitamin D supplements (10–20 mcg/400-800 IU, per day) lowered the risk of death from all causes in people over 50 years old, many of whom had low vitamin D status to start with, though only by a modest amount i.e. 7 per cent. Further effects have been described in the regulation of the immune system (e.g. in autoimmune diseases such as multiple sclerosis and rheumatoid arthritis), blood pressure, congestive heart failure, chronic kidney disease, muscle function and an improvement in type II diabetes.

| Vitamin D | |
| --- | --- |
| Target intake... | 2–4 portions of oily fish per week plus other dietary sources of vitamin D (see table on page 48) |
| Good source of... | 8mcg |
| Source of... | 2mcg |

**Recommendations**

Although the evidence linking vitamin D to a reduced risk of prostate cancer is weak and only seems to apply to men with vitamin D deficiency (less than 40 nmol/L), sufficient vitamin D is essential for good health. Many people with dark skin or living in northern latitudes have deficient vitamin D status that can be improved through diet. If you fall into these categories, we recommend the intake of two to four portions of oily fish per week, and the regular consumption of foods fortified with vitamin D (margarine, fortified breakfast cereals, fortified milk and orange juice in the US). If you do not think you can achieve this intake from diet, you may wish to consider supplementing, particularly in the winter when you have no sun exposure, but we recommend that you should not go above current UK/US guidelines of 10–15mcg per day and on no account should you exceed 25mcg (1,000 IU) per day.

The summary table on page 39 details our suggested target intake and our definition of a 'good source of' and 'a source of' that has been included in the recipes.

# vitamin E

Vitamin E is the collective term for a group of eight similar chemicals made by plants. Vitamin E is essential for human health and has important antioxidant roles as well as apparently beneficial effects on the risk of various disorders such as atherosclerosis, heart disease and cancer. Of the eight forms of vitamin E, alpha-tocopherol (the form found in supplements) is by far the most biologically active, while gamma-tocopherol has other important protective functions. Though inconsistent and limited, there is evidence to suggest that vitamin E may have a protective role in prostate cancer development and progression.

**Evidence from human studies**

A number of studies have assessed the effects of vitamin E on prostate cancer risk. Some assessed vitamin E intake from diet or supplements while others measured the amount of vitamin E circulating in the blood. Findings have varied with some studies showing a benefit associated with higher levels of vitamin E intake or blood levels and others showing no effect. Most studies that assessed vitamin E intake found that supplements, rather than high intakes from food alone, appeared to have the greatest effect. It was noticeable that the benefits were stronger in smokers than in non-smokers and for advanced prostate cancer rather than total prostate cancer. The studies that assessed blood levels

Health Study, published in December 2008, found no effect of supplements of synthetic alpha-tocopherol [267mg (400IU) on alternate days] or vitamin C (500mg per day) on prostate-cancer risk. However, a major difference between the two studies was the very small number of participants who smoked, so if the effect of vitamin E is predominantly in smokers, according to the authors, it would likely have been missed in that trial.

### How does vitamin E work?

Vitamin E is best known for its antioxidant activities which enable it to protect cells and DNA from damage. Vitamin E has been shown to inhibit the growth of various types of cells, to reduce tumour growth in mice, to cause prostate cancer cells to die and to reduce levels of testosterone, a hormone which is required for the growth of prostate cancer cells. Although alpha-tocopherol is generally considered the most potent form of vitamin E, gamma-tocopherol has unique protective effects including reduction of inflammation, suggesting that it may potentially be more important in protection from prostate cancer.

### Vitamin E intake

In the UK there are no specific guidelines for ideal intakes of vitamin E, although a minimum of 4mg per day for men and 3mg per day for women is thought to be adequate. In 2004, average intake in the UK, excluding supplement intake, was 10.6mg per day for men, with little variation between age groups. These levels are more than enough for general health but fall well below

of vitamin E were more inconsistent in their findings but again indicated that smokers may gain more benefit than non-smokers. Interestingly, one study showed that gamma-tocopherol appeared to have more benefit than alpha-tocopherol.

The strongest evidence for a protective effect of vitamin E on prostate cancer risk comes from the ATBC (Alpha-Tocopherol Beta-Carotene) trial carried out in Finland and published in 1998.

In the trial, 29,133 male smokers were given supplements of either alpha-tocopherol (50mg or 75 IU), beta-carotene, neither, or both for approximately six years to test their effect on lung-cancer risk. In the group that took the alpha-tocopherol supplements, there were 32 per cent fewer prostate cancer cases and 41 per cent fewer deaths from prostate cancer. Notably, the supplements appeared to protect from the spread of tumours beyond the prostate gland. By contrast, the US Physicians' the 50mg per day and over that were reported in studies using supplements. While alpha-tocopherol is the usual form in supplements and in European diets, gamma-tocopherol is quantitatively the largest vitamin E component in the US diet. It should be noted that high doses of alpha-tocopherol reduce the level of blood and tissue gamma-tocopherol, a potentially undesirable effect.

## Sources

Vitamin E is made by plants and is fat-soluble; this means that it is found predominantly in the fats and oils of plants. Good sources of vitamin E include wheatgerm, vegetable oils and margarine, nuts and nut oils, seeds such as sunflower seeds and some legumes including soya beans and chickpeas (see table on page 48). Other good sources include egg yolk, Parmesan and Cheddar cheese, oatmeal, olives, avocados, carrots, green leafy vegetables, sweet potatoes, tomatoes and watercress. In addition, some cereals are fortified with vitamin E. Fat spreads, cereals and cereal products make important contributions to vitamin E intakes in the UK.

## Other benefits of vitamin E

Vitamin E may have protective effects against cancers in other sites including oesophageal (gullet), gastric, lung and colorectal cancers. It is also thought to reduce the risk of atherosclerosis and heart disease, partly because it can limit the oxidation of fats in the body.

## Risk of excessive vitamin E intake

Levels of vitamin E up to 1,000mg

(1500 IU) per day can normally be tolerated without causing harm, although increased blood-clotting times have been seen above 400mg (600 IU) per day in some people. This effect on clotting time may explain the increased risk of haemorrhagic stroke seen in some studies where vitamin E supplements were given. Long-term use of 268mg (400 IU) vitamin E supplements by patients with diabetes or poor blood flow through the arteries was linked to increased risk of heart failure and death. Supplementation with high dosages of vitamin E could also interfere with medicinal drugs, potentially reducing the benefits of drug therapy.

## Recommendations

While some studies indicate a protective role of vitamin E, in general findings are inconsistent and far from conclusive. The evidence of a beneficial effect of vitamin E is strongest for smokers and at supplemental levels, rather than from high intakes from food alone. An additional intake of as little as 10mg per day is likely to be sufficient to raise the concentration of vitamin E in the blood to a level associated with protection. Changing diet can be effective as shown by a study in which people were put on a diet rich in rapeseed oil, a readily available and inexpensive cooking oil that is a good source of gamma-tocopherol. At the end of three weeks, their blood levels of gamma-tocopherol had increased by 23 per cent, while those of alpha-tocopherol had risen by 7 per cent.

We recommend trying to increase intake of vitamin E through dietary

means. Smokers may want to consider vitamin E supplements but they would be well advised to look for a low-dose supplement, ideally no more than 50mg (75 IU) per day (as in the ATBC trial). Given the time for vitamin E to be cleared from the system, it would probably be equally good to take a 100mg supplement (which may be easier to find) every other day. Try to find a vitamin E supplement that contains mixed tocopherols which will contain gamma-tocopherol as well. Those on medication should consult their doctor before supplementing and should not go above a dose of 134mg (200 IU) per day.

None of the recipes here will be termed a 'good source' because few foods contain particularly high amounts of vitamin E and those that do are high in fat which would increase the calorie and fat content of the recipe if large amounts were to be used. We have termed recipes that contain 3mg or more per serving a 'source of' vitamin E, as this is a relatively high amount to have in one meal.

# foods to consume in limited amounts

Inevitably, when research is carried out into the links between diet and prostate cancer, some foods or food components will show a positive relationship. This means that eating them in large amounts may actually increase the risk of prostate cancer. The foods that have been suggested as having a positive relationship include dairy products, fat and meat.

## dairy products

Dairy products include milk and all products made from milk, such as yogurt, cheese and fromage frais. The evidence for an association between prostate cancer and dairy products comes from population studies. Although most studies seem to show an association with increased risk of prostate cancer, there are some that show no association or even a decreased risk, although these have mainly been carried out on population groups with moderate or low intake of dairy foods. The explanations for the proposed increased risk of prostate cancer from dairy products have generally focused on their content of calcium and phytanic acid.

### Calcium

Dairy products provide our main source of calcium and some studies have shown a relationship between high intakes of calcium and increased prostate cancer risk. One of the reasons suggested for this increased risk is the relationship between calcium and vitamin D, a potential anti-cancer agent. Calcium requires the action of vitamin D to aid its absorption. Therefore when calcium intakes are high, the demand for vitamin D increases and may lead to the suppression of vitamin D in the blood.

The relationship between an increased risk of prostate cancer and calcium appears to be most apparent when calcium intake is very high (1,500–2,000mg per day) and in cases where the disease is more advanced, although the evidence is not consistent. Interestingly, studies that have considered the risk of prostate cancer with non-dairy sources of calcium appear to show no association, although the effect of calcium supplementation is unclear.

### Phytanic acid

Phytanic acid is a fatty acid found in dairy products and in ruminant animal meat such as beef and lamb. A small study showed that the amount of phytanic acid in the blood of prostate cancer patients was higher than that in the blood of people without prostate cancer. This same study also showed that the blood levels of phytanic acid in this group of people were related to the amounts of dairy foods and red meat in their diets. A role for phytanic acid in the development and progression of prostate cancer was therefore suggested.

The effect of phytanic acid on prostate cancer risk has also been linked to the over-expression of a gene in prostate cancer cells that is responsible for the breakdown of phytanic acid. This has led to speculation that prostate-cancer cells may use this fatty acid as an energy source which can help them to grow.

### Current guidelines for the consumption of dairy foods

Dairy foods represent a major food group that is widely consumed and encouraged as part of a healthy balanced diet. Healthy eating guidelines (the UK 'Eatwell Plate' and the US 'MyPyramid' food pyramid) recommend that dairy foods should make up about one sixth of the food eaten by adults each day in the UK or one fifth of the food eaten by adults each day in the US. This equates to 568ml (about one pint) or 732ml (three cups) of milk or the equivalent in a combination of dairy foods such as 189–244ml (one third of a pint to one cup) of milk, plus 120g or one cup (245g) of yogurt and 28–42g of cheese. This intake would provide between 700 and 1,000mg of calcium per day which meets the recommended calcium intake for the adult population in many countries and provides most of the recommended intake in the countries that have set a higher target.

### Recommendations

The current guidelines for the consumption of dairy foods should not increase the risk of prostate cancer. However, the evidence does seem to suggest a possible association with high intakes. Therefore those who regularly consume quantities greater than the recommended intakes should consider substituting some of their intake with non-dairy alternatives such as soya products (not calcium-fortified) which have been suggested as having a beneficial effect on prostate cancer. While dairy products provide one of the best sources of calcium, there are a number of other good dietary sources including dark-green leafy vegetables such as spinach and kale, oily fish with bones such as sardines and dried apricots, all of which can be included in a healthy and varied diet.

If a decision is made to undertake a dairy-free diet, it should only be done with advice from a qualified dietitian. Dairy products are a major source of calcium and iodine, and supplementation should be considered if they are not supplied in sufficient quantities in the diet. Calcium is essential for bone health which could be compromised in men receiving hormone therapy resulting in a greater risk of osteoporosis (softening of the bones). It is therefore important that these men follow the advice of their doctor regarding the prescription of calcium supplements.

Considering the possible association of high intakes of dairy foods with prostate cancer, the majority of the recipes in this book are dairy-free, contain only a little dairy, or give options for the inclusion of dairy-free alternatives. Where possible, the dairy component of the recipe is replaced with soya to provide more of the beneficial ingredients.

## fat

A high intake of fat has been identified as a key contributor to non-communicable diseases such as heart disease. Its relationship with prostate cancer also appears to be a detrimental one. In countries where fat intake is relatively low, there appears to be a low risk of prostate cancer. Research has generally supported the association between high intakes of fat, particularly saturated or animal fats, and increased risk of prostate cancer, across a range of ethnic groups. Diets high in fat are also likely to be high in calories, thereby promoting obesity which is associated with more aggressive prostate cancer and prostate cancer mortality. Encouragingly, some studies have suggested that low-fat diets may slow the progression of prostate cancer, particularly to the hormone-independent stage. While the general message is to choose low-fat foods, especially those low in saturated or animal fats, there are some high-fat foods, such as oily fish, that are probably beneficial and should be included in a diet aimed at prostate health.

### Effects of different types of fat
Dietary fat can be divided into different types of fatty acids including saturated fatty acids, monounsaturated fatty acids (MUFA) and polyunsaturated fatty acids (PUFA). The PUFA group has further sub-groups, the omega-6 and omega-3 fatty acids.

The omega-3 fatty acid group includes the long-chain PUFAs from fish oils that appear to offer some protection against prostate-cancer progression and death (see Fish section). Alpha-linolenic acid is an omega-3 fatty acid of plant origin that has been suggested to be detrimental to prostate cancer risk. In the US, important sources of alpha-linolenic acid are margarine, butter, mayonnaise, oil- and vinegar-based and creamy salad dressings, beef, pork and lamb. However, some studies have shown no association with alpha-linolenic acid or even a decreased risk.

Diets high in omega-6 fatty acids may promote the growth of cancer cells, probably because they are converted to inflammatory compounds that can stimulate tumour growth. Linoleic acid, which is found in most vegetable oils and margarines, is the most common omega-6 PUFA in the Western diet, accounting for 8.9 per cent of energy intake (compared to 0.8 per cent in the Far East) and makes a significant contribution to total fat intake.

There is some suggestion that intake of MUFA, found in foods such as olive oil, rapeseed oil and avocados, is associated with an increase in prostate cancer risk, although when olive oil is looked at specifically, the effect appears to be protective, perhaps because olive oil has other beneficial components. Saturated fatty acids which are predominantly from animal sources, such as the fat on meat, appear to be the fatty acid group most associated with an increase in prostate cancer risk.

Although the mechanisms linking fat and its various components to prostate cancer risk are unclear, effects on testosterone levels, insulin-like growth-factor-1 (a promoter of prostate cancer growth), and inflammation, a factor known to contribute to prostate cancer risk, may well be involved.

### Recommendations

As the evidence relating to a detrimental effect of specific fatty acids is unclear, the current recommendations for fat intake which are also beneficial for heart health provide the most appropriate guideline for prostate health. Total fat intake should constitute no more than 25–35 per cent of total energy intake, with saturated fat being limited to 10 per cent of total energy intake. Ways to help achieve this include choosing lean cuts of meat, removing any excess fat, removing the skin from poultry, as well as choosing oils and spreads that are higher in polyunsaturated fatty acids and particularly omega-3 fatty acids and monounsaturated fatty acids such as olive oil. For instance you could replace butter with olive spread or an omega-3 spread, use rapeseed oil for frying and olive oil for salads. By making these changes, you will not only be reducing the intake of saturated fat but also the intake of omega-6 fatty acids which are associated with undesirable inflammatory effects.

## meat

There is some evidence that diets high in meat, particularly red and processed meats, may increase the risk of prostate cancer. In a 2001 review of 22 studies, 16 of them showed a 30 per cent or more increased risk associated with meat intake. By contrast, the 2007 World Cancer Research Fund/American Institute for Cancer Research (WCRF/AICR) review of diet and cancer found that no conclusions could be drawn on the relationship between prostate-cancer risk and meat in general, though there was some evidence to support an increase in risk from eating processed meat.

Because results are inconsistent, it has been suggested that other dietary components associated with meat may be possible promoters or inhibitors of risk. For instance meat intake has also been associated with high fat intake which, as we have discussed, may also have cancer-promoting effects. Furthermore, diets high in meat may also be low in protective fruits and vegetables. Ruminant meats, such as beef and lamb, are also a source of phytanic acid, which has been linked to an increase in the risk of prostate cancer in the case of dairy produce. Red meat is a major source of zinc which promotes testosterone synthesis. Perhaps more importantly, the way in which meat is often cooked can lead to the formation of undesirable cancer-causing compounds.

A number of studies have compared the relationship between the degree of meat cooking and prostate cancer risk. Meat that is 'well done' and 'very well done' is more likely to increase the risk of prostate cancer. When muscle meats are cooked at high temperatures, a group of substances known as heterocyclic amines can be formed. Heterocyclic amines have been listed as substances 'reasonably anticipated to be human carcinogens' by the US Department of Health and Human Services. Other cooked animal foods such as eggs, milk and organ meats (i.e. liver and kidney) contain only very small amounts of heterocyclic amines. Furthermore, cooking on charcoal grills can deposit polycyclic hydrocarbons, which are known to cause cancer, on the outside of the meat.

### Recommendations

To help prevent and control cancers, the WCRF/AICR recommend consuming less than 500g (18 oz) per week of red meat, only a little of which should be processed meat. While this is a reasonable target, it is important to note that meat is part of a valuable food group that provides protein to build and repair body tissues, as well as many essential vitamins and minerals, such as iron. There are of course other sources of protein such as fish, eggs, soya and pulses that can substitute for some meat. If a decision is taken to remove meat from the diet completely, it should be done only after careful consideration of the nutritional content of the diet as a whole and ideally with the advice of a dietitian.

The US National Cancer Institute (NCI) offers the following advice to reduce the formation of heterocyclic amines when cooking meat: 'Concerned individuals can reduce their exposure to heterocyclic amines by varying methods of cooking meats, microwaving meats more often, especially before frying, grilling (broiling), or barbecuing; and refraining from making gravy from meat drippings'. In line with these recommendations, we have for the most part included recipes where meat is cooked in a sauce to try to limit the formation of heterocyclic amines and no meat is barbecued. Furthermore, a number of the recipes have used reduced serving sizes of meat or suggest how this may be achieved.

## Foods to consume in limited amounts – examples

| **Dairy Products** | **Saturated Fat** | **Red and Processed Meat*** |
|---|---|---|
| Cheese | Biscuits | Beef |
| Cheese sauce | Butter | Pork |
| Cheesecake | Cakes | Lamb |
| Condensed milk | Coconut cream | Goat |
| Cream | Coconut oil | Bacon |
| Crème caramel | Cream | Frankfurters ('Hot dogs') |
| Crème fraîche | Crème fraîche | Ham |
| Custard | Desiccated coconut | Hamburgers |
| Dried milk | Ghee | Pastrami |
| Evaporated milk | Hard cheese | Salami |
| Flavoured milk | Lard | Sausages |
| Fromage frais | Meat fat | |
| Ice cream | Meat pies | *defined by WCRF/ AICR 2007* |
| Milk | Meat products | |
| Milkshake | Palm oil | |
| Mousse | Pastry | |
| Rice pudding | Salami | |
| Semolina | Sausages | |
| Soured cream | Soured cream | |
| Tzatziki | | |
| White sauce | | |
| Yogurt | | |

## Suggested intakes for dairy foods, dietary fat and meat

| | |
|---|---|
| **Dairy foods...** | No more than 568ml (1 pint) *or* 732ml (3 cups) of milk *or* the equivalent in dairy foods (see text for more details) |
| **Dietary fat...** | Total fat should not be more than 25–35 per cent of total energy intake Saturated fat should not be more than 10 per cent of total energy intake |
| **Meat...** | No more than 500g per week of red meat to include only a little processed meat Avoid burnt meat, and cooking meat at high temperatures e.g. barbecuing |

## Sources of the foods and food components beneficial for prostate cancer

| Food | Amount per 100 g | Portion size (g) | Amount per portion |
|---|---|---|---|
| **Lycopene** | | | |
| Tomato juice | 9.0 mg | 160 | 14.4 mg |
| Tomato soup | 5.3 mg | 220 | 11.7 mg |
| Watermelon | 4.5 mg | 200 (large slice) | 9.0 mg |
| Tomato paste | 28.8 mg | 15 (1 tbsp) | 4.3 mg |
| Tomato purée | 21.8 mg | 15 (1 tbsp) | 3.3 mg |
| Tomato ketchup | 15.2 mg | 20 | 3.0 mg |
| Guava | 5.4 mg | 55 | 3.0 mg |
| Papaya | 2.0–5.3 mg | 140 (average slice) | 2.8–7.4 mg |
| Tinned tomatoes | 2.8 mg | 100 | 2.8 mg |
| Tomatoes (raw) | 2.6 mg | 85 (1 medium) | 2.2 mg |
| Pink grapefruit | 1.4 mg | 125 (½ medium) | 1.8 mg |
| Sundried tomatoes | 45.9 mg | 2 (1 piece) | 0.9 mg |
| Baked beans | 0.5 mg | 135 | 0.7 mg |
| Dried apricots | 0.9 mg | 40g (5 apricots) | 0.4 mg |
| **Vitamin E** | | | |
| Sunflower seeds | 37.8 mg | 16 (1 tbsp) | 6.0 mg |
| Salmon | 3.9 mg | 100 | 3.9 mg |
| Pecan nuts | 26.7 mg | 14 (10 halves) | 3.8 mg |
| Almonds | 24.0 mg | 13 (6 whole) | 3.1 mg |
| Sardines (tinned in tomato sauce) | 3.1 mg | 90 | 2.8 mg |
| Sweet potato | 4.6 mg | 65 (1 medium) | 3.0 mg |
| Hazelnuts | 25.0 mg | 10 (10 whole) | 2.5 mg |
| Avocado | 3.2 mg | 75 ( ½ pear) | 2.4 mg |
| Tinned tuna (in oil) | 1.9 mg | 92 | 1.8 mg |
| Brazil nuts | 14.4 mg | 12 (3 nuts) | 1.7 mg |
| Sunflower oil | 49.2 mg | 3 (1 tsp) | 1.5 mg |
| Spinach | 1.7 mg | 90 | 1.5 mg |
| Peanuts | 10.1 mg | 13 (10 whole) | 1.3 mg |
| Wheatgerm | 22.0 mg | 5 (1 tbsp) | 1.1 mg |
| Palm oil | 33.1 mg | 3 (1 tsp) | 1.0 mg |
| Tomatoes | 1.2 mg | 85 (I medium) | 1.0 mg |
| Walnuts | 3.9 mg | 20 (6 halves) | 0.8 mg |
| Margarine | 7.9 mg | 10 (on slice of bread) | 0.8 mg |
| Eggs | 1.1 mg | 61 (I size 2) | 0.7 mg |
| Soya bean oil | 18.2 mg | 3 (1 tsp) | 0.6 mg |
| Peanut oil | 15.6 mg | 3 (1 tsp) | 0.5 mg |
| Mango | 1.1 mg | 40 (1 slice) | 0.4 mg |
| Pine nuts | 11.2 mg | 1.7 (10 nuts) | 0.4 mg |
| Sesame seeds | 2.5 mg | 12 (1 tbsp) | 0.3 mg |
| Olive oil | 5.1 mg | 3 (1 tsp) | 0.2 mg |

| Food | Amount per 100 g | Portion size (g) | Amount per portion |
|---|---|---|---|
| **Vitamin D** | | | |
| Herring | 16.1 mcg | 119 | 19.2 mcg |
| Trout | 9.6 mcg | 155 | 14.9 mcg |
| Mackerel | 8.8 mcg | 160 | 14.1 mcg |
| Pilchards (tinned in tomato sauce) | 14.0 mcg | 100 | 14.0 mcg |
| Salmon | 7.1 mcg | 100 | 7.1 mcg |
| Sardines (tinned in tomato sauce) | 8.0 mcg | 100 | 8.0 mcg |
| Shiitake mushrooms (sun-dried) | 41.5 mcg | 10 | 4.2 mcg |
| Tuna (tinned in oil) | 3.0 mcg | 92 | 2.8 mcg |
| Eggs | 1.8 mcg | 61 (I size 2) | 1.1 mcg |
| Margarine | 7.9 mcg | 10 (on slice of bread) | 0.8 mcg |
| Fortified breakfast cereals | 2.8–8.3 mcg | 30 | 0.8–2.5 mcg |
| Butter | 0.9 mcg | 10 (on slice of bread) | 0.1 mcg |
| **Selenium** | | | |
| Kidney lamb/pig | 150 mcg | 112 | 168 mcg |
| Brazil nuts (NB very variable content) | 1530 mcg | 12 (3 nuts) | 153 mcg |
| Lemon sole | 60 mcg | 170 | 102 mcg |
| Tuna (tinned in oil) | 90 mcg | 92 | 83 mcg |
| Swordfish | 45 mcg | 140 | 63 mcg |
| Lobster | 41 mcg | 150 | 62 mcg |
| Mackerel | 30 mcg | 160 | 48 mcg |
| Liver (lamb) | 42 mcg | 100 | 42 mcg |
| Sardines (tinned) | 41 mcg | 100 | 41 mcg |
| Pork | 34 mcg | 120 | 40 mcg |
| Crab | 37 mcg | 85 | 32 mcg |
| Sardines (fresh) | 34 mcg | 86 (6 sardines) | 29 mcg |
| Chicken | 12 mcg | 150 | 18 mcg |
| Duck | 12 mcg | 150 | 18 mcg |
| Pheasant | 16 mcg | 110 | 17 mcg |
| Turkey (light meat) | 10 mcg | 150 | 15 mcg |
| Prawns | 16 mcg | 60 | 10 mcg |
| Eggs | 11 mcg | 61 | 7 mcg |
| Cashew nuts | 20 mcg | 20 | 4 mcg |

*These figures are taken from the United States Department of Agriculture, McCance and Widdowson's 'The Composition of Foods' and a number of scientific studies.*

# Sources of the foods and food components beneficial for prostate cancer

## *Allium* Vegetables
Chives
Garlic
Leeks
Onion
Spring onions (scallions)
Shallots

## Cruciferous Vegetables
Bok choy (Pak choi)
Broccoli
Brussels sprout
Cabbage
Cauliflower
Garden cress
Horseradish
Kale
Mustard
Radish
Rocket
Turnip (swede)
Wasabi
Watercress

## Oily fish
Anchovies
Bloater
Carp
Eel
Herring
Kipper
Mackerel
Pilchard
Salmon
Sardines
Sprats
Swordfish
Trout
Tuna
Whitebait

## Phytoestrogens
### Soya (soy)
Meat alternatives, e.g. soya bacon, sausages and burgers
Miso soup
Natto (an Asian food)
Soya beans ('Edamame', available frozen or dried)
Soya cereal
Soya cheese
Soya custard
Soya dip
Soya flour
Soya ice cream
Soya and linseed bread
Soya milk
Soya nuts (roasted soya beans)
Soy pasta
Soya protein
Soy sauce
Soya spread
Soya yogurt
Tempeh (an Asian food)
Tofu (soya bean curd)

## Legumes
Beans, e.g. broad, black, haricot, white, pinto, kidney, aduki
Chickpeas
Lentils
Peanuts
Peas

## Lignans
Cashew nuts
Cranberries
Flaxseed (linseed)
Peanuts
Raisins
Rye (bran)

## Polyphenols
Green tea
Pomegranate fruit
Pomegranate juice
Raspberries
Strawberries

breakfasts

# blueberry smoothie

This smoothie is easy to prepare and makes a refreshing start to the day. A bonus is that blueberries boost your concentration.

SERVES 2

- 150g blueberries
- 2 x 125ml raspberry-flavoured soya yogurts
- soya or rice milk to dilute

Put the blueberries and yogurt in a blender and whizz until smooth.

Blend in enough milk to reach the desired consistency.

*Good source of soya. Source of vitamin E*
PER PORTION: 148 KCAL, 3.6G FAT, 0.7G SATURATED FAT

# pomegranate and guava smoothie

This smoothie makes a great snack at any time of the day.

SERVES 2

- 410g tin guavas, drained and deseeded
- 1 medium ripe banana
- 300ml pomegranate juice, plus extra to loosen

Put the fruit and juice in a blender and whizz until smooth.

Blend in a little extra pomegranate juice to reach the desired consistency.

*Good source of polyphenols. Source of lycopene*
PER PORTION: 221 KCAL, 0.2G FAT, 0.1G SATURATED FAT

# porridge with raspberry and pomegranate compote

This is a warming breakfast that is quick to make. The compote can be made a day or so in advance and refrigerated until ready to use. This dish has been adapted from a recipe on www.alprosoya.co.uk.

SERVES 1

**For the Compote**
- 80g fresh or frozen raspberries (thawed)
- 50ml pomegranate juice
- honey to taste

**For the Porridge**
- 50g porridge oats
- 250ml soya milk
- honey to taste

To make the compote, place the raspberries and the pomegranate juice in a saucepan. Bring to the boil and simmer for 5 minutes or until the liquid has reduced. Remove from the heat and stir in honey to taste.

To make the porridge, place the oats and milk in a medium-sized heatproof bowl and stir. Cook on full power in the microwave for 2 minutes, stir and cook for a further minute. Leave to stand for 1 minute and stir in the honey to taste.

Loosen the consistency with more milk if preferred and top with the compote.

*Good source of polyphenols and soya. Source of vitamin E*
PER PORTION: 363 KCAL, 8.4G FAT, 1.5G SATURATED FAT

# salmon kedgeree

This Indian-style breakfast makes a wonderful brunch to share with friends.

SERVES 4

- 400g salmon fillets
- 1 tablespoon lemon juice
- 2 tablespoons and ½ teaspoon olive oil
- salt and pepper
- 3 eggs
- 275g basmati rice
- ½ red chilli or more to taste
- ½ teaspoon turmeric
- ½ teaspoon garam masala
- 4 tablespoons fresh parsley, chopped
- yogurt or soya yogurt to serve (optional)

Preheat the oven to 150°C/300°F/gas 2.

Wash the salmon fillets and place on a sheet of tin foil. Sprinkle with the lemon juice, ½ teaspoon olive oil, salt and pepper and let it sit for a few minutes.

Wrap the fish in the foil and cook in the oven for 15–20 minutes or until cooked through, then break into large flakes. Meanwhile, boil the eggs in water for 10 minutes until hard-boiled. Drain, peel and chop into 1–2cm pieces. Boil the rice for 10 minutes and drain.

Heat 2 tablespoons of olive oil in a pan and lightly stir-fry the chilli for 30 seconds. Add the turmeric and heat, stirring, for 1–2 minutes. Remove the pan from the heat, add the rice, and stir into the turmeric until the rice is a soft yellow colour.

Stir in the salmon, eggs, garam masala and most of the parsley. Serve with yogurt and sprinkled with the remaining parsley.

*Good source of oily fish. Source of selenium*
PER PORTION: 579 KCAL, 24.7G FAT, 4.6G SATURATED FAT

# bagels with oven-roasted tomatoes and rocket

Oven-roasting cherry tomatoes gives them a wonderful, concentrated flavour. You can do this the day before if you prefer, ready to serve for breakfast the next day. This dish has been selected from www.eggrecipes.co.uk.

SERVES 4

- 450g cherry tomatoes, halved
- 1 tablespoon olive oil
- 4 large eggs
- 4 bagels, split
- large handful of wild rocket leaves
- salt and freshly ground black pepper

Preheat the oven to 150°C/300°F/gas 2.

Place the tomatoes cut side up on a baking tray, drizzle over the oil and season. Bake for 35–40 minutes or until the tomatoes have shrivelled and dried out a little.

Fill a large frying pan with salted water and bring to the boil. Carefully crack the eggs into the simmering water then reduce the heat and cook for 3–5 minutes depending how you like your eggs cooked. Lift the eggs from the water with a slotted spoon and drain on kitchen paper.

Meanwhile, toast the bagels. To serve, place each bagel on a plate. Top with tomatoes, rocket and a poached egg.

Season to taste and serve straight away.

*Source of cruciferous vegetables and lycopene*
PER PORTION: 317 KCAL, 10.6G FAT, 2.4G SATURATED FAT

# sun-dried shiitake mushroom and tomato omelette

This omelette makes a satisfying cooked breakfast and is great served with wholemeal toast and baked beans.

SERVES 1

- 10g sun-dried shiitake mushrooms, soaked in warm water according to packet instructions
- 10g olive spread
- 6g sun-dried tomatoes in oil, drained and chopped
- 2 eggs
- 1 tablespoon water
- salt and pepper

Preheat the grill to hot.

Drain and slice the mushrooms and remove any hard stalks. Melt the spread in a frying pan. Add the mushrooms and sauté until golden brown. Add the tomatoes and heat through.

Meanwhile, whisk together the eggs and water, and season with salt and pepper. Add the egg mixture to the mushrooms and tomatoes, and stir gently.

Draw the set mixture from the sides of the frying pan into the middle and allow the liquid mixture to run to the sides. When the omelette has set, place the frying pan under the hot grill to brown the top.

*Source of lycopene, vitamin D, vitamin E and selenium*
PER PORTION: 290 KCAL, 22.1G FAT, 5.6G SATURATED FAT

# apricot and brazil nut breakfast bars

These delicious breakfast bars are easy to make and can be kept in the fridge for days to grab as a quick breakfast or healthy snack. The Brazil nuts provide plenty of selenium, and as there is no added fat, they are healthier than most cereal bars.

MAKES 14

- 150g dried apricots
- 150g Brazil nuts
- 50g dark chocolate chips
- 50g rolled oats
- 50g muesli
- 30g puffed rice cereal
- 3 tablespoons golden syrup
- 5 tablespoons orange juice

Preheat the oven to 180°C/350°F/gas 4.

Chop the dried apricots and Brazil nuts into small pieces of irregular size. Place all the dry ingredients in a mixing bowl and mix well. Next, stir in the golden syrup and orange juice until evenly combined.

Line a swiss-roll tin (20cm x 30cm) with greaseproof paper and spoon in the mixture. Smooth down with the back of a spoon so the mixture is tightly packed and of even thickness.

Place in the oven for 20 minutes; check after 15 minutes to ensure it does not burn. Remove from the oven and leave to cool for an hour or two, then chill in the fridge overnight.

Cut into 14 bars and store in the fridge.

*Good source of selenium*
PER BAR: 162 KCAL, 9.0G FAT, 2.4G SATURATED FAT

# cranberry and brazil nut breakfast bars

These are an equally tasty variation of the Apricot and Brazil Nut Breakfast Bars.

MAKES 14

- 150g dried cranberries
- 150g Brazil nuts
- 50g rolled oats
- 50g muesli
- 30g puffed rice cereal
- 3 tablespoons golden syrup
- 5 tablespoons pomegranate or apple juice

Preheat the oven to 180°C/350°F/gas 4.

Chop the dried cranberries and Brazil nuts into small pieces of irregular size. Place all the dry ingredients in a mixing bowl and mix well. Next, stir in the golden syrup and fruit juice until evenly combined.

Line a swiss-roll tin (20cm x 30cm) with greaseproof paper and spoon in the mixture. Smooth down with the back of a spoon so the mixture is tightly packed and of even thickness.

Place in the oven for 20 minutes; check after 15 minutes to ensure it does not burn. Remove from the oven and leave to cool for an hour or two, then chill in the fridge overnight.

Cut into 14 bars and store in the fridge.

*Good source of selenium*
PER BAR: 158 KCAL, 8.0G FAT, 1.8G SATURATED FAT

soups,
starters
and dips

# caribbean pepperpot

Garnished with peppers, this soup is vibrant, fragrant and colourful. It is also packed with beneficial vegetables. This recipe has been selected from *The New Cranks Recipe Book* by Nadine Abensur.

SERVES 4

- 5 tablespoons sunflower oil
- 150g onions, diced
- 3 garlic cloves, finely chopped
- 300g potatoes, diced
- ½ teaspoon bouillon powder, dissolved in 250ml hot water
- 100g white cabbage, diced
- 400g tin chopped tomatoes
- 1 heaped tablespoon paprika
- 1 heaped teaspoon ground coriander
- dash of Tabasco
- ½ teaspoon ground chilli powder
- 1 fresh chilli, finely chopped
- 400ml tin coconut milk
- pinch of soft brown sugar (optional)

*For the Peppers*
- 1 tablespoon sunflower oil
- 1 red pepper, diced
- 1 yellow pepper, diced
- dash of Tabasco
- 1–2 tablespoons tamari (wheat-free soy sauce)

Heat the oil and sauté the onions and garlic until transparent.

Add the diced potatoes until they too are transparent. Add 4 tablespoons of the hot bouillon, stir and cook for 1 minute or so. Then add the diced cabbage and sauté for 2–3 minutes. Drain the chopped tomatoes, reserving the juice. Add the tomatoes to the soup together with the paprika, ground coriander, Tabasco and chilli powder. Stir well and add a further 150ml of the hot bouillon, the reserved tomato juice and fresh chilli. Simmer gently for 7–8 minutes and add the coconut milk.

Check the sweetness of the soup and, if necessary, add a pinch of soft brown sugar. For the peppers, heat the oil in a frying pan and sauté the diced peppers for just a minute, until they begin to blacken in places. Add a drop or two of Tabasco and tamari to taste and set aside.

To serve, mix half the peppers into the soup and reserve the rest to use as garnish on each serving or in the soup tureen.

*Good source of* Allium *vegetables. Source of cruciferous vegetables, lycopene and vitamin E*
PER PORTION: 332 KCAL, 20.9G FAT, 3.1G SATURATED FAT

# armenian soup

This soup has a wonderful and unusual flavour and goes well with the Peanut and Linseed Bread (page 76). This recipe has been kindly provided by Jo Dilley.

SERVES 4

- 55g red lentils, washed
- 55g ready-to-eat dried apricots
- 1 medium potato, chopped
- 1.2 litres vegetable stock
- juice of half a lemon
- 1 teaspoon ground cumin
- salt and pepper
- 3 tablespoons fresh parsley plus extra sprigs to serve
- 4 tablespoons yogurt or soya yogurt (optional) to serve

Put all the ingredients except the yogurt and the extra sprigs of parsley into a large pan and bring to the boil. Reduce the heat, cover and simmer for 30 minutes.

Leave the soup to cool, then whizz in a food-processor or blender until smooth. Reheat and adjust seasoning to serve.

Garnish each bowl with a swirl of yogurt and a sprig of parsley.

*Source of legumes*
PER PORTION: 137 KCAL, 2.7G FAT, 0.2G SATURATED FAT

# broad bean soup

Serve this delicious summer soup with crusty home-made bread. You can substitute the broad beans with peas if you prefer. This recipe has been kindly provided by Dr John Rayman.

SERVES 4–6

- 2 tablespoons olive oil
- 1 bunch of spring onions, chopped
- 500g frozen or fresh broad beans
- 20g parsley, chopped
- 400ml full-fat soya milk
- salt and pepper
- pinch of nutmeg
- soya cream to serve (optional)

If the broad beans are large, with tough outer skins, blanch them for 1 minute and drain. Then pop them out of their skins and simply continue with the recipe as follows.

Heat the oil in a saucepan and gently cook the spring onions until they are soft. Add the beans and parsley and just enough water to cover the beans. Bring to the boil, cover and simmer for 5–10 minutes or until the beans are cooked.

Allow the soup to cool and then blend to a purée in a food-processor or blender. In a clean pan, stir the purée into the milk and heat gently without boiling. Add salt, pepper and nutmeg to taste. Serve with a swirl of soya cream if desired.

*Good source of legumes. Source of* **Allium** *vegetables and soya*
PER PORTION: 171 KCAL, 10G FAT, 1.5G SATURATED FAT

# chilled tomato bisque

This recipe has been kindly provided by Antony Worrall Thompson. It is based on gazpacho but is smooth instead of chunky. It is wonderfully refreshing on a hot summer's day.

SERVES 4

- 1 slice wholemeal bread, crusts removed and broken into large crumbs
- 1 tablespoon sherry vinegar
- 1 garlic clove, peeled and finely chopped
- 1 teaspoon caster sugar
- ½ red chilli, deseeded and finely diced
- 30ml extra virgin olive oil
- 400g tin tomatoes
- 200ml tomato juice
- 2 spring onions, finely sliced
- ½ red pepper, roasted or grilled, peeled, deseeded and diced
- ½ large cucumber, peeled, deseeded and roughly diced
- 1 dessertspoon pesto
- salt and freshly ground black pepper

Place the bread in a food-processor or blender. With the machine running add the vinegar, garlic, sugar and chilli, and blend until smooth. Add the extra virgin olive oil until the bread will absorb no more then, a little at a time, add the tomatoes, tomato juice, spring onions, red pepper, cucumber and pesto.

Continue to blend to form a smooth emulsion. Season to taste with salt and black pepper and transfer to a large bowl. Ladle into chilled soup bowls and serve immediately.

*Good source of lycopene. Source of* **Allium** *vegetables*
PER PORTION: 138 KCAL, 9.1G FAT, 1.5G SATURATED FAT

# roasted tomato and sweet potato soup

Roasting the tomatoes and sweet potato enhances their beautiful flavours. Serve this delicious soup with Brazil Nut, Tomato and Onion Bread (page 74).

SERVES 4

- 450g sweet potatoes, peeled and sliced
- 1.2kg tomatoes, halved
- 2 tablespoons olive oil
- 1 large onion, chopped into wedges
- 2 garlic cloves, sliced
- salt and pepper
- 1 small bunch basil leaves, torn, plus extra to garnish
- 1 tablespoon tomato purée

Preheat the oven to 200°C/400°F/gas 6.

Parboil the potatoes in a saucepan for 5 minutes, drain and leave to cool. Place all the ingredients except for the tomato purée on a roasting tray and drizzle with the oil.

Roast in the oven for 30 minutes, turning the vegetables halfway through. Once removed from the oven, pick any burnt skins off the tomatoes which will come away easily.

Whizz all the ingredients along with 600ml water and the tomato purée in a blender or food-processor. Reheat to serve and garnish with a few basil leaves.

*Good source of* Allium *vegetables and lycopene. Source of vitamin E*
PER PORTION: 236 KCAL, 7.9G FAT, 1.4G SATURATED FAT

# winter vegetable soup

For this heart-warming soup, why not try varying the vegetables? You could use parsnips, cabbage, or whatever you fancy, but keep the leeks and onion to get a good source of *Allium* vegetables.

SERVES 6

- 30g olive spread
- 2 leeks, sliced
- 2 carrots, peeled and chopped
- 1 potato, peeled and chopped
- 1 swede, peeled and chopped
- 1 onion, chopped
- 2 tablespoons fresh herbs, chopped
- 1.4 litres vegetable or chicken stock
- salt and pepper

Melt the olive spread in a large pan and add all the ingredients except the stock. Cover and heat gently for 20 minutes, stirring occasionally. Add a few tablespoons of water if the vegetables begin to stick, then add the stock, cover and simmer for a further 10 minutes or until the vegetables are tender.

Leave to cool and put in a food-processor or blender and whizz until smooth. Season with salt and pepper to taste. You may want to set aside a few pieces of the chopped, cooked vegetables to garnish. Reheat to serve.

*Good source of* Allium *vegetables. Source of cruciferous vegetables*
PER PORTION: 91 KCAL, 4.2G FAT, 0.7G SATURATED FAT

# watercress soup

The watercress gives this soup a lovely peppery taste which works well with the dairy-free cream. This dish has been adapted from a recipe on www.alprosoya.co.uk.

SERVES 4

- 1 medium onion, finely chopped
- 1 tablespoon olive oil
- 250g new potatoes
- 2 large bunches of watercress
- 400ml vegetable stock
- 250ml dairy-free alternative to single cream

Fry the onion in the olive oil until soft. Add the peeled and chopped potatoes and cook for 2 minutes. Add the watercress and pour on the boiling stock.

Bring back to the boil and then simmer for 15–20 minutes until the potatoes are cooked. Blend the soup while adding the cream, reserving 1 tablespoon for serving. Adjust seasoning and serve with a swirl of cream to finish.

**Source of Allium *and cruciferous vegetables and soya***
PER PORTION: 226 KCAL, 6.4G FAT, 2.2G SATURATED FAT

# tiger prawn and shiitake mushroom broth

This recipe was created by TV chef Alex Mackay. Here's what he has to say about it:

*'This very pretty soup is both fresh and refreshing, with a little bite from the ginger and a fresh burst of mint at the end. Prawns are delightful with soy, somehow standing up to the strength of the sauce and soothing it at the same time. The peppers and honey help too, giving the soup a gentle suggestion of sweetness.'*

SERVES 4

- 12 whole tiger prawns, head and shell on
- 2 lemon grass sticks, finely chopped
- 3 tablespoons grated ginger (no need to peel it)
- 2 tablespoons tomato paste
- 2 tablespoons soy sauce
- 2 tablespoons honey
- 1.5 litres chicken stock (or vegetable bouillon)
- 2 small red peppers, cut in half, deseeded and chopped into small chunks
- 4 garlic cloves, peeled and chopped
- 1 bunch of spring onions, roots trimmed and sliced on an angle
- 12 sun-dried shiitake mushrooms, soaked and thickly sliced
- 2 heads of pak choi, cut into quarters
- 180–200g medium egg noodles (2 of the squares from a packet)
- 5 sprigs of mint leaves, picked from their stalks and sliced

Remove the shells and heads from the prawns and put them into a large saucepan. Remove the veins from the prawn tails and set aside. Add the lemon grass, ginger, tomato paste, soy sauce, honey and stock to the prawn heads and shells in the pan. Bring to the boil and simmer rapidly for 15 minutes.

Strain the stock into a clean pan. Add the peppers and garlic. Bring to the boil, lower the heat and simmer for 5 minutes. Bring a large pan of water to the boil for the noodles. Add the prawns, salad onions, mushrooms and pak choi to the stock and poach gently for 5–6 minutes making sure the liquid never boils. Boil the noodles for 3–4 minutes and strain into a colander. Scoop into soup plates and top with the prawns, vegetables and mint. Boil the broth and ladle it over the top.

**Good source of Allium *and cruciferous vegetables. Source of lycopene and vitamins E and D***
PER PORTION: 364 KCAL, 6.1G FAT, 1.5G SATURATED FAT

# pea and mint soup

This pretty, bright green soup should be blended well for a smooth and creamy texture. It makes a satisfying lunch served with crusty bread. This recipe has been kindly provided by Dr John Rayman.

SERVES 4

- 175g onions, chopped
- 150g potatoes, diced
- 1 tablespoon olive oil
- 1.2 litres vegetable (or chicken) stock
- 450g frozen petits pois, defrosted
- 1 bunch of mint, chopped
- 300ml soya milk
- salt and pepper
- a little soya cream and a few mint leaves to garnish

Sweat the onion and potato in the olive oil for 5 minutes until soft (but not browned). Add the stock, bring to the boil and simmer for 20 minutes or until the potato is soft. Add the peas, bring back to the boil and simmer for 2 minutes.

Add the mint and then immediately purée in a blender until the soup is smooth. Add the soya milk. Season with salt and pepper and then reheat gently before serving.

Garnish with a swirl of soya cream and a few mint leaves.

**Good source of legumes. Source of Allium vegetables and soya**
PER PORTION: 184 KCAL, 6.8G FAT, 0.9G SATURATED FAT

# roasted cauliflower and carrot soup

Roasting the vegetables brings out the sweet flavours in this thick and creamy soup.

SERVES 6

- 250g carrots, peeled and chopped
- 2 tablespoons olive oil
- salt and pepper
- 540g cauliflower, chopped into florets
- 3 garlic cloves, chopped
- 1 medium onion, chopped
- 1.25 litres vegetable or chicken stock
- 1 teaspoon grated nutmeg
- paprika to serve

Preheat the oven to 180°C/350°F/gas 4.

Place the carrots on a roasting tray, toss in half a tablespoon of the oil and sprinkle with salt and pepper. Roast for 10 minutes. Remove from the oven, add the cauliflower florets and another half tablespoon of oil to the tray. Return to the oven for a further 20 minutes.

Meanwhile heat the remaining tablespoon of oil in a pan over a medium heat and cook the garlic and onions for 5 minutes. Pour in the stock and simmer for 5 minutes. Finally, add the roasted vegetables and nutmeg, and simmer for a further 5 minutes.

Remove from the heat and leave to cool, then blend until smooth. Reheat and sprinkle with paprika to serve.

**Good source of cruciferous vegetables. Source of Allium vegetables**
PER PORTION: 103 KCAL, 6.1G FAT, 1.0G SATURATED FAT

# french onion soup

This hearty soup is marvellous on a cold and wet autumn evening. This recipe has been kindly provided by Dr John Rayman.

SERVES 4

- 1kg onions, sliced
- 1 tablespoon olive oil
- 1 litre beef stock
- salt and pepper

**For the Croutons**
- 2 garlic cloves, crushed
- 1 tablespoon olive oil
- 4 slices stale bread, crusts removed, cut into 1cm cubes
- Gruyère cheese, grated, to serve (optional)

Preheat the oven to 200°C/400°F/gas 6.

Sweat the onions gently in the olive oil in a large saucepan until they are golden brown. Add the stock and season with salt and pepper. Bring to the boil and simmer, covered, for about 45 minutes.

To make the croutons, fry the garlic and bread in the olive oil in a frying pan for a couple of minutes.

Turn the contents of the frying pan on to a baking sheet and place in the oven for about 10 minutes or until the croutons are browned. Serve the soup topped with the croutons and some grated Gruyère if desired.

**Good source of Allium vegetables**
PER PORTION: 122 KCAL, 4.7G FAT, 0.5G SATURATED FAT

# brazil nut, tomato and onion bread

This bread has a lovely texture and is great with soup. Try sprinkling other seeds on the top of the loaves such as cumin, caraway or fennel. This bread also freezes very well. The recipe has been kindly provided by Dr John Rayman.

MAKES 10 SLICES PER LOAF

- 3 medium onions, chopped
- 2 tablespoons olive oil
- 75g Brazil nuts, chopped
- 50g sun-dried tomatoes, chopped
- 300g wholemeal rye flour
- 450g strong white bread flour
- 2 teaspoons salt
- 1 packet dried yeast
- 450ml water
- milk for glazing
- 4 teaspoons poppy seeds

Preheat the oven to 220°C/425°F/gas 7.

Fry the onions gently in the olive oil in a frying pan until they are soft and light brown. Place the nuts, tomatoes, flours, salt and yeast in the bowl of a food-processor (using a dough hook if you have one) and tip in the entire contents of the frying pan. Mix for a few seconds to blend in the oil.

Mix 150ml of boiling water and 300ml of cold water and add to the mixture. Process, or knead by hand, until you have a smooth dough. You may need to add a little more water at this stage; don't worry if the dough becomes a little sloppy. Put the dough into a large bowl, cover with cling film and leave in a warm place until the volume of the dough has doubled.

Grease two 450g loaf tins. Knead the dough briskly for a few minutes. Divide the dough into two equal parts and place each half in a loaf tin. Cover the tins with cling film and leave until the volume of the dough has doubled again. Brush the loaves with milk and sprinkle the poppy seeds on top. Put the loaves into the hot oven and bake for 30 minutes. Remove the loaves from the baking tins and bake for another 10 minutes or until a skewer stuck into the bread comes out clean. Leave to cool on a wire rack.

**Good source of selenium. Source of Allium vegetables and lycopene**
PER SLICE: 186 KCAL, 6.3G FAT, 1.1G SATURATED FAT

# peanut and linseed bread

Although this recipe only meets our criteria as a source of vitamin E, it contains legumes (peanuts) and phytoestrogens as lignans (linseeds and rye). To give the bread a coarser texture, you can replace some of the white flour with granary or wholemeal flour, or add a tablespoon of seeds to the flour mixture. This bread freezes very well.

MAKES 10 SLICES PER LOAF

- 100g salted peanuts, chopped coarsely
- 80g linseeds, briefly milled in a grinder
- 150g sunflower seeds
- 200g wholemeal rye flour
- 550g strong white bread flour
- 1 tablespoon olive oil
- 2 teaspoons salt
- 1 packet dried yeast
- 450ml water
- milk for glazing
- 4 teaspoons caraway seeds
- sunflower, sesame, pumpkin, or hemp seeds (optional)

Preheat the oven to 220°C/425°F/gas 7.

Process the peanuts briefly in a food-processor to give a coarse ground mixture. Grind the linseeds in a coffee grinder for 10–15 seconds. Place the peanuts, linseeds, sunflower seeds, flours, olive oil, salt and yeast in the bowl of a food-processor (using a dough hook if you have one). Mix to blend in the oil. Mix 150ml of boiling water and 300ml of cold water and add to the mixture. Process or knead until you have a smooth dough. You may need to add a little more water; don't worry if the dough becomes a little sloppy.

Put the dough in a large bowl, cover with cling film and leave in a warm place until the volume of the dough has doubled. Grease two 450g loaf tins. With floured hands, knead the dough briskly for a few minutes, then divide into two equal parts and place each half in a loaf tin. Cover the tins with cling film and leave until the dough volume has doubled again. Brush the loaves with milk and sprinkle the caraway seeds on top. Put the loaves into the oven and bake for 30 minutes. Remove the loaves from the baking tins and bake for another 10 minutes or until a skewer stuck into the bread comes out clean. Leave to cool on a wire rack.

*Source of vitamin E*
*PER SLICE: 235 KCAL, 9.9G FAT, 1.3G SATURATED FAT*

# broad bean and apple crostini

Crostini are great as an appetizer or as a lunch dish with salad. For an attractive appetizer plate serve these with the Sweet Tomato and Chilli Crostini (opposite page).

SERVES 4–6

- 1 small French stick cut into 12 slices about 2cm thick
- 1 tablespoon olive oil

*For the Broad Bean and Apple Topping*
- 200g frozen broad beans
- 1 tablespoon crunchy peanut butter
- 1–2 tablespoons water
- 4 spring onions, sliced
- 1 small red apple, diced
- salt and pepper

Preheat the oven to 200°C/400°F/gas 6.

Brush the bread slices on both sides with the olive oil and place on a baking tray. Place in the oven for about 10 minutes or until the bread is golden brown. Remove from the oven and leave to cool.

Cook the broad beans in boiling water for about 5 minutes. Drain and set aside until cool enough to handle. Remove the skins from the broad beans and discard. Place two thirds of the broad beans in a bowl and mash with a fork. Mix in the peanut butter and enough water to make a soft paste.

Stir in the remaining broad beans, spring onions and apple, and season to taste. Spread a generous amount of topping on each of the bread slices and serve.

*Source of legumes*
*PER PORTION: 290 KCAL, 10.9G FAT, 1.8G SATURATED FAT*

# sweet tomato and chilli crostini

The sweet chilli sauce works well with the tomatoes in this recipe. For an attractive appetizer plate serve these with the Broad Bean and Apple Crostini (opposite page).

SERVES 4–6

- 1 small French stick cut into 12 slices about 2cm thick
- 1 tablespoon olive oil

### For the Tomato and Chilli Topping
- 1 teaspoon olive oil
- 1 small red onion, finely chopped
- 2 garlic cloves, crushed
- 40g sun-dried tomatoes, finely chopped
- 2 fresh tomatoes, chopped
- 2 teaspoons sweet chilli sauce, or more to taste
- salt and pepper

Preheat the oven to 200°C/400°F/gas 6.

Brush the bread slices on both sides with the olive oil and place on a baking tray. Place in the oven for about 10 minutes or until the bread is golden brown. Remove from the oven and leave to cool.

Heat the oil for the topping in a small frying pan, add the onion and garlic and cook until soft. Next add the sun-dried tomatoes and continue to cook for a further couple of minutes. Remove from the heat and leave to cool. Put the chopped tomatoes in a bowl and stir in the onion mixture. Add the sweet chilli sauce, stir to combine and season to taste. Heap a generous mound of topping on to each bread slice and serve.

*Good source of lycopene. Source of* **Allium** *vegetables and vitamin E*
PER PORTION: 270 KCAL, 11.7G FAT, 1.8G SATURATED FAT

# dr john's liver terrine

This is a dish of Ashkenazi Jewish origin, traditionally served with Jewish unleavened bread known as matzos. It can be served with additional onions browned in olive oil and allowed to cool. You can decorate it with chopped hard boiled eggs. Chicken livers can be substituted for some of the lamb's liver, and the proportions of liver, egg and onion can be adjusted to taste. This recipe has been kindly provided by Dr John Rayman.

SERVES 10

- 650g lamb's liver, sliced
- 500ml chicken stock
- 5 medium eggs
- 1 tablespoon olive oil
- 500g onions, chopped
- salt and pepper

In a saucepan gently poach the liver in the chicken stock until it is cooked. Remove from the heat and leave to cool in the pan. Hard boil the eggs by boiling them in water for 10 minutes, drain and leave to cool, then remove the shells.

Heat the oil in a frying pan and fry the onions until golden brown, remove from the heat and leave to cool in the pan. Either mince the eggs, liver and onion together using a hand mincer or alternatively use a food-processor in short pulses to produce a rough-textured terrine, not a smooth pâté.

Season to taste with salt and pepper and enough of the chicken stock to ensure that the terrine is moist.

*Source of Allium vegetables and selenium*
PER PORTION: 165 KCAL, 8.8G FAT, 2.2G SATURATED FAT

# POM salsa

This pomegranate salsa is excellent served with tortilla chips and will keep covered in the fridge for 2 to 3 days. The recipe has been selected from www.pomwonderful.com.

SERVES 4

- 2–3 large pomegranates
- 50ml pomegranate juice
- 3–4 teaspoons jalapeño pepper, chopped
- 40g yellow pepper, finely chopped
- 4 tablespoons coriander, chopped
- 1 tablespoon granulated sugar
- 1 tablespoon rice vinegar

Score 2–3 fresh pomegranates and place in a bowl of water.

Break open the pomegranates under water to free the arils (red seed sacs). The arils will sink to the bottom of the bowl and the membrane will float to the top. Sieve the arils and put them in a separate bowl. Leftover arils can be refrigerated or frozen to use another time. Put all the ingredients in a large bowl and thoroughly mix to combine.

*Good source of polyphenols*
PER PORTION: 71 KCAL, 0.3G FAT, 0.0G SATURATED FAT

# cooked tomato salsa

This salsa is good served warm or chilled and makes a great accompaniment to cooked meats and salad.

SERVES 4

- 1 tablespoon olive oil
- 1 bunch of spring onions, sliced
- 2 garlic cloves, chopped
- 400g tomatoes, chopped
- juice of half a lime
- 1 teaspoon sugar
- salt and pepper

Gently heat the olive oil in a frying pan. Add the onions and garlic, and lightly cook for about 5 minutes until the onions are soft and golden.

Add the tomatoes and cook for a further 5 minutes. Add the lime juice and sugar and continue cooking for a further 1–2 minutes.

Season to taste and serve or chill in the fridge for later.

*Source of* **Allium** *vegetables and lycopene*
PER PORTION: 60 KCAL, 3.9G FAT, 0.6G SATURATED FAT

# broad bean purée

This fresh broad bean recipe is taken from *Moro: The Cookbook* by Sam and Sam Clark. It was inspired by the classic, earthy Egyptian fava bean purée (made with dried broad beans). Serve as a starter with pitta bread or as part of a mezze.

SERVES 4

- 1kg fresh broad beans, podded (or 300g already podded)
- 1 garlic clove, crushed to a paste with salt
- a squeeze of lemon
- 2 tablespoons olive oil
- 1 small bunch of fresh mint, roughly chopped
- sea salt and black pepper

Bring a saucepan of unsalted water to the boil and add the fresh podded broad beans. Cook for about 5 minutes or until soft.

Drain, then transfer to a food-processor or mouli and purée until smooth. Transfer to a bowl, then add the garlic, lemon juice, olive oil and mint, and season with salt and pepper. If the texture is a little thick, we suggest stirring in some extra oil or water.

*Source of* **Allium** *vegetables and legumes*
PER PORTION: 141 KCAL, 7.9G FAT, 1.1G SATURATED FAT

salads

# chickpea salad

This salad can be served as part of a mixed salad plate or as an accompaniment to fish or poultry. This recipe has been kindly provided by Suzanne Burton.

SERVES 4–6

- 225g bulgar wheat, prepared according to packet instructions
- 50g dried apricots, finely chopped
- 1 red onion, finely chopped
- 400g tin chickpeas, drained and rinsed
- 50g sun-dried tomatoes in oil, drained and chopped
- 1 bunch of spring onions, sliced
- 1 large handful of coriander, chopped
- 85g pitted black olives
- 4 tablespoons sunflower seed kernels
- salt and pepper

*For the Dressing*
- juice of 1 lemon
- 2 tablespoons olive oil
- 2 garlic cloves, crushed

Put the prepared bulgar wheat in a large bowl. Stir in the remaining salad ingredients, except the seasoning. Combine the dressing ingredients and stir into the salad. Season to taste.

*Good source of legumes and lycopene. Source of* Allium *vegetables, vitamin E and selenium*
PER PORTION: 525 KCAL, 20.5G FAT, 2.3G SATURATED FAT

# greek salad

This is a pretty-looking salad which couldn't be easier to make. It can be served as a light, summery side dish and makes a welcome addition to a buffet.

SERVES 6

- 4 tomatoes
- 1 red onion
- 1 cucumber
- 150g feta cheese
- 400g tin chickpeas, drained
- 1 tablespoon mint sauce or a handful of fresh mint, chopped

Chop the tomatoes, onion, cucumber and feta cheese into cubes of uniform size, about the size of a chickpea. Place all the ingredients in a large bowl and mix well.

*Source of* Allium *vegetables, legumes and lycopene*
PER PORTION: 132 KCAL, 6.5G FAT, 3.6G SATURATED FAT

# salmon vermicelli salad

This dish was kindly provided by Dr Sophie Chen, Research Director of the Ovarian and Prostate Cancer Research Trust Laboratory. It is really tasty and packed with beneficial ingredients.

SERVES 2

- 50g dry vermicelli, rice or mung bean noodles
- 80g carrots, shredded
- 160g mung bean sprouts
- 80g watercress or rocket
- 2 salmon fillets, grilled or baked
- 20g shredded crispy seaweed

**For the Sauce**
- 2 tablespoons olive oil
- 2 tablespoons balsamic vinegar
- 2 tablespoons soy sauce
- 3–4 garlic cloves, chopped
- ½ teaspoon sesame oil (optional)
- 1 tablespoon lemon juice (optional)

Prepare the vermicelli according to the packet instructions, cut into shorter pieces and place in a large bowl. Add the carrot and mung bean sprouts.

Combine the sauce ingredients in another bowl and mix well. Add two thirds of the sauce to the vermicelli mixture and put aside. Layer the watercress or rocket on to a plate, followed by a layer of the vermicelli mixture.

Place the salmon on top of the vermicelli salad and pour over the remaining sauce. Finally, sprinkle over the crispy seaweed.

*Good source of Allium vegetables, oily fish, legumes and vitamin D. Source of cruciferous vegetables, selenium and vitamin E*
PER PORTION: 494 KCAL, 27.2G FAT, 4.7G SATURATED FAT

# mediterranean pasta salad

This colourful dish is a real taste of the Mediterranean and goes down a treat as part of a buffet. As well as tasting great, the sun-dried tomatoes will give you a big dose of lycopene!

SERVES 10–20

- 500g pasta bows
- 4 tablespoons olive oil
- 1 tablespoon white wine vinegar
- 1 tablespoon tomato purée
- 1 tablespoon red pesto
- 1 small jar sun-dried tomatoes in olive oil, drained and chopped
- handful of pitted black olives, halved
- a few basil leaves, shredded

Boil the pasta according to the packet instructions and drain.

Mix together the oil, white wine vinegar, tomato purée and red pesto and stir into the pasta. Simply combine with the remaining ingredients and serve at room temperature.

*Good source of lycopene*
PER PORTION: 264 KCAL, 9.1G FAT, 1.3G SATURATED FAT

# asian salad

This is a delightful, crunchy salad full of beneficial foods. The tofu provides a good source of soya, but if you prefer you could use cooked chicken breast instead.

SERVES 4

- a few handfuls of salad leaves
- 3 large tomatoes
- 1 cucumber, peeled and cut into wedges
- 1 head broccoli, chopped into very small florets
- ½ red pepper, cut into thin strips
- 2 medium onions, cut into fine rings
- 3 hard-boiled eggs, chopped into wedges
- half a bunch coriander
- 320g tofu, cubed

*For the Dressing*
- 80g unsalted, roasted peanuts
- 120ml (½ cup) lemon juice
- 3 tablespoons white wine vinegar
- 4 garlic cloves
- 3 tablespoons chopped coriander and stalks
- 3 tablespoons sugar
- 1 teaspoon salt
- 1 tablespoon water
- 1 whole chilli
- 1 tablespoon fish sauce

For the dressing, whizz all the ingredients together in a blender or food-processor. Pour into a large bowl.

Place the salad leaves on four plates and toss all of the other salad ingredients into the dressing. Lay the salad on the bed of leaves and serve.

*Good source of Allium and cruciferous vegetables and soya. Source of lycopene, legumes and vitamin E*
PER PORTION: 383 KCAL, 19.2G FAT, 3.8G SATURATED FAT

# mixed bean salad

With a variety of different beans, this salad, which can be prepared in five minutes, is a tasty way to top up on legumes.

SERVES 6

- 160g frozen baby broad beans
- 100g French beans (fine beans)
- 400g tin mixed beans, drained
- 100g tin sweetcorn, drained
- 1 tablespoon olive oil
- 1 dessertspoon white wine vinegar
- 1 tablespoon wholegrain mustard

Boil the broad beans and French beans in a pan of water for 5 minutes or until cooked. Drain and leave to cool.

Mix all the ingredients in a bowl and serve.

*Good source of legumes*
PER PORTION: 100 KCAL, 3.1G FAT, 0.4G SATURATED FAT

# POM vinaigrette

As only a small quantity of vinaigrette is used to dress a salad, this recipe does not meet any of our 'source of' or 'good source of' criteria. However, it is an excellent way to serve up some extra pomegranate juice and *Allium* vegetables. This vinaigrette can be made up to two days before serving and kept in the fridge. This recipe has been selected from www.pomwonderful.com.

MAKES ABOUT 240ML

- 80ml pomegranate juice
- 60g pomegranate arils (optional)
- 60ml olive oil
- 80ml red or white wine vinegar
- 2 tablespoons grated red onion
- ½ teaspoon sugar, or to taste
- ½ teaspoon salt
- ⅛ teaspoon freshly ground pepper

In a screw-top jar or a plastic container with a tight-fitting lid, combine all of the dressing ingredients. Cover and shake well. Set aside or refrigerate before serving.

PER PORTION (2 TABLESPOONS): 76 KCAL, 7.5G FAT, 1.1G SATURATED FAT

# tiger prawn salad with mango and avocado

Look for the largest, freshest tiger prawns in the fish market – they need little cooking and taste divine. This dish has been selected from *Gordon Ramsay Makes It Easy* by Gordon Ramsay.

SERVES 2

- 12 raw tiger prawns, peeled, heads removed
- 1 large ripe mango, peeled
- 1 large ripe avocado, peeled
- juice of half a lemon
- 1 tablespoon olive oil
- 1cm piece fresh root ginger, peeled
- 1 garlic clove, peeled
- juice of 1 lime
- sea salt and pepper
- 1 tablespoon flat-leaf parsley, chopped

De-vein the prawns if necessary. Whizz half the mango flesh in a blender or small food-processor to a purée and set aside. Dice the rest of the mango.

Halve and slice the avocado, remove the stone. Arrange the slices around the outside of a small platter and drizzle over the lemon juice. Heat the oil in a large frying pan, add the ginger and garlic and cook for 30 seconds.

Add the prawns and stir-fry for 2–3 minutes until they turn pink – don't overcook. Drizzle with the lime juice and take off the heat. Discard the ginger and garlic.

Add the diced mango to the prawns and toss together. Season with salt and pepper to taste. Pile the prawns and mango on to the middle of the platter and scatter over the parsley. Drizzle the mango purée around the edge of the plate and serve.

*Source of selenium and vitamin E*
PER PORTION: 365 KCAL, 26.3G FAT, 5.1G SATURATED FAT

# salad niçoise

This French-style salad is delicious served with a crusty French baguette.

SERVES 4

- 2 eggs, raw
- 320g potatoes
- 100g French beans
- 300g tuna steaks
- 1 teaspoon olive oil
- salt and pepper
- 100g rocket
- 4 tomatoes, cut into quarters
- 1 small onion, chopped or thinly sliced
- 20g tin anchovy fillets in oil, drained
- handful of black olives

*For the Dressing*
- half a small bunch of fresh basil
- 1 garlic clove
- 2 tablespoons fresh lemon juice
- 4 tablespoons olive oil
- salt and pepper

Preheat the grill to hot.

Boil the eggs in water for 10 minutes until hard-boiled. Drain and leave to cool. Peel and cut into sixths. In another pan boil the potatoes for 20 minutes or until tender, adding the French beans for the last 5 minutes. Drain the potatoes and beans and run under the cold tap.

Chop the potatoes into bite-size pieces. Brush the tuna with 1 teaspoon of olive oil and rub with salt and pepper. Grill for about 2 minutes on each side. Leave to stand for a few minutes and cut into cubes. To make the dressing, lower the basil leaves in a sieve into one of the pans of boiling water for a few seconds until wilted, then run under a cold tap. Blend the dressing ingredients together using a hand-held blender or food-processor.

In a serving bowl, toss together the potatoes, beans, rocket, tomatoes, onion and most of the dressing. Lay the egg and tuna on top, followed by the anchovies, then sprinkle with the olives and drizzle with the remaining dressing.

*Good source of selenium. Source of* **Allium** *and cruciferous vegetables, legumes, lycopene, oily fish and vitamin E*
378 KCAL, 22.7G FAT, 4.3G SATURATED FAT

# cauliflower and broccoli salad

This salad can be served with couscous, warm pasta bows, or as part of a combined salad plate. Olives can be added too – just stir them in at the end. This dish has been selected from *The New Cranks Recipe Book* by Nadine Abensur.

SERVES 6

- 1 large cauliflower, separated into florets
- 500g broccoli, separated into florets
- 2 red peppers, chargrilled, peeled and thinly sliced

*For the Dressing*
- 100ml extra-virgin olive oil
- 1 heaped tablespoon grain mustard
- 15g fresh tarragon, picked off the stalks
- 4 garlic cloves, finely crushed
- dash of Tabasco
- dash of balsamic vinegar
- salt and freshly ground black pepper

Plunge the cauliflower and broccoli florets into a pan of salted boiling water and blanch for 1 minute until tender but still firm. Meanwhile combine the dressing ingredients.

Combine all the salad ingredients in a bowl and pour the dressing over them while the cauliflower and broccoli are still hot. Add more grain mustard to taste if necessary.

*Good source of cruciferous vegetables. Source of* **Allium** *vegetables*
PER PORTION: 222 KCAL, 18.8G FAT, 2.8G SATURATED FAT

main courses

# tuna stir-fry

This is a quick and easy meal to make. Try experimenting with different fish e.g. salmon, and a variety of different beneficial vegetables. This dish has been adapted from a recipe by Jamie Oliver on www.sainsburys.co.uk.

SERVES 4

- 400g fresh tuna steaks
- 3 tablespoons soy sauce
- 5cm piece fresh ginger, peeled and grated
- small bunch of coriander, finely chopped, keep some for garnish
- 2 fresh chillis, deseeded and finely chopped
- 100g dried egg noodles
- 1 teaspoon sesame oil
- 1 tablespoon rapeseed oil, plus a little extra to cook the tuna
- 4 spring onions, finely sliced
- 1 garlic clove, peeled and finely sliced
- 1 carrot, peeled and stripped with a peeler
- handful of sugar snap peas, sliced lengthways
- 1 red pepper, cut into strips
- ½ Chinese cabbage, thinly sliced
- large handful of fresh bean sprouts

Place the tuna in a plastic bag with the soy sauce, ginger, coriander and one of the red chillis, seal and refrigerate for at least 20 minutes. Cook the noodles according to the packet instructions, rinse with cold water, drain well and toss in the sesame oil.

Remove the tuna to kitchen paper and reserve the marinade. Rub the tuna lightly with a little rapeseed oil. Heat the griddle and place the tuna in when hot. Cook on each side for 1–2 minutes, transfer to a plate and keep warm.

Heat the rapeseed oil in a wok. Add the spring onions and garlic, and cook for a few seconds. Add the carrot, sugar snap peas, red peppers, cabbage and bean sprouts. Stir-fry until slightly softened. Add the noodles and warm through. Add the leftover marinade and cook for a few seconds. Sprinkle with coriander to serve.

*Good source of oily fish and selenium. Source of* **Allium** *vegetables, cruciferous vegetables, legumes and vitamin D*
PER PORTION: 332 KCAL, 11.2G FAT, 2.3G SATURATED FAT

# tuna fish cakes

These fish cakes are very simple and taste wonderful whether you use salmon or tuna. They go down a treat served with a burger bun, tomato ketchup and salad.

SERVES 6

- 600g potatoes, peeled and chopped
- 2 tablespoons olive oil
- 1 medium onion, grated
- 1 chilli, finely chopped (or to taste)
- 1 teaspoon dried thyme
- 2 rashers of bacon, finely chopped
- 600g fresh tuna (or salmon)
- 1 egg, beaten
- salt and pepper
- flour for dusting

Boil the potatoes in a pan of water for 20 minutes or until tender. Drain and mash the potatoes. Heat 1 tablespoon of the oil in a frying pan and gently fry the onion, chilli, thyme and bacon for about 10 minutes or until the onions are soft. Set aside and leave to cool.

Coarsely mince the fish flesh with a knife or in a food-processor. Mix all the ingredients together. Dust your hands with a little flour to avoid the mixture sticking to your hands and form into cakes. The mixture can either be made into 12 patties or into fish balls to serve as a starter.

On a low heat, lightly fry the fish cakes on each side in the remaining tablespoon of oil for about 15 minutes, turning once. If making into patties, serve 2 each.

*Good source of oily fish, selenium and vitamin D. Source of* **Allium** *vegetables*
PER PORTION: 304 KCAL, 11.6G FAT, 2.6G SATURATED FAT

# festival mackerel

This interesting dish was kindly provided by Al Crisci who is the Catering Manager at High Down Prison, Surrey. He was the winner of the 'dinner lady' category of the BBC Food and Farming Awards in 2005. It is traditionally served with a 'festival' (a deep-fried baton-shaped dough dumpling) but can equally well be served with focaccia or crusty French bread.

SERVES 4

- 1 large onion, peeled and roughly chopped
- 1 tablespoon olive oil
- ½ large white cabbage, core removed and thinly sliced
- 400g tin chopped tomatoes
- 2 tablespoons tomato purée
- 2 garlic cloves, chopped
- 1 teaspoon chilli, or to taste
- 400g smoked mackerel fillets, skinned and flaked

Gently fry the onion in the olive oil until soft but not brown. Add the cabbage and mix well. Continue cooking until the cabbage wilts. Add the tomatoes, tomato purée, garlic, chilli, and about 60ml of water. Cook until the cabbage is tender, adding some more water if it starts to dry out. When the cabbage is cooked and most of the liquid has evaporated, stir in the flaked mackerel and continue to heat until the mackerel is hot. Add some seasoning at the end if required.

*Good source of cruciferous vegetables, oily fish and vitamin D.*
*Source of Allium vegetables, lycopene, selenium and vitamin E*
PER PORTION: 463 KCAL, 35.8G FAT, 6.8G SATURATED FAT

# devilled mackerel with mint and tomato salad

This dish was kindly provided by John Walter, Head Chef at the University of Surrey's Lakeside Restaurant. The fresh tangy salad carries off the spices and oily fish beautifully.

SERVES 4

- pinch of cayenne pepper
- 1 teaspoon paprika
- 1 teaspoon ground coriander
- 1 teaspoon finely ground black pepper
- 1 teaspoon English mustard powder
- 1 teaspoon caster sugar
- salt
- 40ml olive oil
- 2 tablespoons red wine vinegar
- 640g mackerel fillets

*For the Salad*
- 2 beefsteak tomatoes, chopped
- 1 small red onion, peeled and thinly sliced
- handful of fresh mint leaves
- juice of 1 lemon

Preheat the grill to hot. Mix the spices, mustard powder, sugar and a little salt with the olive oil and red wine vinegar.

Carefully remove any remaining bones from the mackerel fillets and with a sharp knife, make three shallow incisions across the skin running down each fillet. Brush the fillets on both sides with the devil marinade and place on a baking tray. Place under a hot grill for about 5 minutes until nicely browned.

To make the salad, combine the tomatoes, onion and mint leaves in a bowl and squeeze over the lemon juice. To serve, pile the salad on to a plate and place the mackerel on top.

*Good source of oily fish, selenium and vitamin D. Source of lycopene*
PER PORTION: 476KCAL, 36.4G FAT, 6.8G SATURATED FAT

# spicy sardines with chickpea and avocado salad

This recipe was kindly provided by TV Chef Antony Worrall Thompson. This lovely salad is full of flavour and works perfectly with the oily fish.

SERVES 4

**For the Chickpea and Avocado Salad**
- yolk of 1 hard-boiled egg, sieved
- 4 tablespoons olive oil
- 2 tablespoons red wine vinegar
- ½ red onion, finely chopped
- 1 garlic clove, crushed
- 2 tablespoons flat-leaf parsley, chopped
- 1 tablespoon small capers, drained and rinsed
- 400g tin chickpeas, drained and rinsed
- 1 ripe avocado, peeled and chopped into chunky dice
- salt and ground black pepper

**For the Sardines**
- 25g olive spread
- 1 fresh red chilli, diced
- 2 shallots, diced
- 1 tablespoon flat-leaf parsley, finely chopped
- 1 tablespoon coriander, finely chopped
- 3 garlic cloves, crushed with a little salt
- 1 tablespoon extra virgin olive oil, plus a little extra for drizzling
- 8 sardines, cleaned, flattened out, backbone removed and washed thoroughly
- juice of 1 lemon

Preheat the oven to 180°C/350°F/gas 4.

To make the salad, place the egg yolk in a bowl, beat in the oil and vinegar and stir in the onion, garlic, parsley, capers, chickpeas and avocado, and season to taste.

To cook the sardines, heat the olive spread in a small pan, add the chilli and shallots and cook until softened but not coloured. Fold in the parsley, coriander, garlic and olive oil; season to taste. Spread the mixture over the flesh side of the fish. Roll up the sardines and secure with 2 small wooden cocktail sticks, (ensure that you have soaked the cocktail sticks in water first, to stop them from burning). Place in the oven and cook for 5–8 minutes. Drizzle with oil and lemon juice and serve two sardine rolls on a pile of salad on each plate.

*Good source of* **Allium** *vegetables and legumes. Source of oily fish, selenium, vitamin D and vitamin E*
PER PORTION: 474 KCAL, 39.8G FAT, 7.3G SATURATED FAT

# prawns in spicy tomato sauce (kimroun bi tamatem)

These prawns are deliciously rich in flavour and are good hot or cold. Serve them with mashed potato or with a little couscous moistened with olive oil. This dish has been selected from *Arabesque* by Claudia Roden.

*Use raw king prawns: they are grey and turn pink when they are cooked. Some supermarkets sell them fresh and ready-peeled. You can also buy them frozen with their heads off from some fishmongers. The weight of these packs is inclusive of a thick ice glaze which means that you need double the weight – i.e. for 500g peeled prawns (about 25), you need a 1kg pack.*

SERVES 6

- 500g raw king prawns, peeled, or 1kg pack frozen prawns
- 1 medium onion, chopped
- 2 tablespoons extra virgin olive oil
- 3 garlic cloves, finely chopped
- 400g tomatoes, peeled and chopped
- half a teaspoon ground ginger
- pinch of saffron threads (optional)
- pinch of chilli pepper
- salt
- bunch of flat-leaf parsley, chopped
- bunch of coriander, chopped

If using frozen prawns, defrost them thoroughly. Pull the legs off the prawns, then peel off the shells and pull off the tails (they are usually sold headless). If you see a dark thread along the back, make a fine slit with a pointed knife and pull it out.

In a large frying pan, fry the onion in the oil, stirring, until it begins to colour. Add the garlic and cook until it begins to colour. Then add the tomatoes, ginger, saffron (if using), chilli pepper and some salt and cook for about 20 minutes until the sauce is reduced. Now put in the prawns and cook them for 3–5 minutes, until they turn pink, turning them over once. Stir in the coriander and parsley at the end.

*Source of* **Allium** *vegetables, lycopene, selenium and vitamin E*
PER PORTION: 125 KCAL, 5.0G FAT, 0.7G SATURATED FAT

# trout and leek paupiette in carrot and coriander sauce

This dish was kindly provided by John Walter, Head Chef at the University of Surrey's Lakeside Restaurant. Serve with green beans and new potatoes for a lovely, light evening meal.

SERVES 4

**For the Fish**
- 1 medium leek, cut in half lengthways to form strips
- ½ teaspoon each of dry-roasted and ground fennel seeds, white peppercorns and sea salt
- 4 skinless trout fillets

**For the Sauce**
- 1 shallot, finely chopped
- 1 teaspoon olive oil
- ½ teaspoon dry-roasted and ground coriander seeds
- 1 large carrot, peeled and finely grated
- 100ml clear fish stock

Preheat the oven to 200°C/400°F/gas 6. Plunge the leek strips into a large saucepan of boiling water and blanch for 2–3 minutes. Drain the leek strips well and divide them into four equal portions. Lay one leek portion flat on a chopping board and spread it out to about the width of one trout fillet.

Combine the trout seasoning ingredients and sprinkle over the trout fillets. Place one seasoned trout fillet on top of the leeks and roll up from end to end. Secure the paupiette with a cocktail stick and place on a lightly oiled baking tray. Repeat this process with each fish and then bake for 10 minutes.

While the trout is cooking, prepare the sauce. Sweat the shallots in the olive oil with the coriander seeds until soft and without colour. Add the carrot and sweat for a further 5 minutes. Pour over the fish stock and blend to a purée. Warm the sauce and season to taste. To serve, cut each trout and leek paupiette in two and serve on a pool of carrot sauce.

*Good source of oily fish and vitamin D. Source of* Allium *vegetables and selenium*
PER PORTION: 227 KCAL, 8.9G FAT, 2.0G SATURATED FAT

# sea bream with sunblush tomatoes and basil

This recipe was kindly provided by TV chef Alex Mackay. Here's what Alex has to say about it:

*'Braising is an excellent way to cook fish, just as healthy as poaching or steaming but much more flavoursome. In this recipe the sea bream has a quick and delightful exchange with the tomato sauce and olive oil, a process that makes everything tastier.'*

SERVES 4

- 1 medium onion, peeled and chopped
- 4 garlic cloves, peeled and sliced
- 3 strips of orange zest (removed with a vegetable peeler)
- 450g very ripe plum tomatoes, cored and roughly chopped or 400g tin chopped tomatoes in juice

- 3 tablespoons and 4 teaspoons extra virgin olive oil
- 2 tablespoons tomato paste
- 20 sunblush tomatoes
- 4 large fillets of sea bream, skin on, scaled
- 25g bunch of basil, leaves picked and sliced
- salt, cayenne pepper and brown sugar

Preheat the oven to 190°C/375°F/gas 5. In a covered saucepan, cook the onion, garlic and orange peel in 3 tablespoons of olive oil over a medium heat until soft, stirring occasionally.

Add the chopped tomatoes and tomato paste along with 100ml water. Bring to the boil and simmer for 15 minutes. Discard the orange zest and season with salt, cayenne and sugar. Add 100ml water and the sunblush tomatoes. Bring to the boil, then transfer the sauce to a shallow ovenproof dish large enough to hold the fish with a little space around the sides. Season the sea bream and spoon a little sauce, followed by one teaspoon of olive oil, over each fillet. Cover with greaseproof paper and braise in the oven for 6 minutes.

Turn off the oven, leave the door ajar and rest the sea bream for 3–4 minutes. Then plate the sea bream, add the basil to the sauce, season to taste and spoon around the fish to serve.

*Good source of Allium vegetables, lycopene and selenium. Source of vitamin E*
PER PORTION: 316 KCAL, 27.3G FAT, 3.6G SATURATED FAT

# tagliatelle with salmon, courgettes and almonds

Freshly cooked pasta served with a salmon and courgette sauce and topped with toasted almonds is a delicious and nutritious meal. It could be accompanied by a mixed dark-green leafy salad. This dish has been adapted from a recipe in *Body and Beauty Foods* by Hazel Courteney and Kathryn Marsden.

SERVES 4

- 25g olive spread
- 225g leeks, washed and thinly sliced
- 225g courgettes, thinly sliced
- 25g plain wholemeal flour
- 425ml vegetable stock
- 150ml dry white wine
- 400g tinned salmon in water, drained and flaked

- 1–2 tablespoons fresh tarragon, chopped
- dash of Tabasco sauce
- salt and freshly ground black pepper
- 350g tagliatelle
- 55g flaked almonds, toasted
- fresh tarragon sprigs, to garnish (or fresh parsley)

Melt the olive spread in a saucepan and add the leeks and courgettes. Cover and cook gently for about 10 minutes, until softened, stirring occasionally.

Add the flour and cook for 1 minute, stirring. Gradually stir in the stock and wine, then bring slowly to the boil stirring continuously until the sauce thickens. Simmer gently for 2 minutes, stirring.

Stir the salmon, chopped tarragon, Tabasco sauce and seasoning into the sauce. Reheat gently until piping hot, stirring. Meanwhile, cook the pasta in a large saucepan of lightly salted, boiling water until *al dente*. Drain the pasta well and transfer to serving plates. Spoon the sauce over the pasta and scatter with almonds. Garnish with the tarragon sprigs.

*Good source of vitamin D. Source of Allium vegetables, oily fish, selenium and vitamin E*
PER PORTION: 616 KCAL, 19.5G FAT, 2.7G SATURATED FAT

# poached salmon steak on spinach and watercress purée

This recipe was kindly provided by chef Raymond Blanc's kitchen. This lovely dish utilises the technique of poaching. The salmon could be replaced by sea trout, turbot, brill or halibut. The stock can be made well in advance and the purée can be prepared 1 hour before you need it and left covered at room temperature.

SERVES 4

- 4 salmon steaks (175g each)

**For the Vegetable Stock**
- 1 medium carrot, peeled and sliced
- 1 small onion, peeled and sliced
- 2 sticks celery, washed and diced
- ½ medium leek, washed and sliced
- 1 strip lemon zest
- bouquet garni (2 sprigs thyme, 1 sprig parsley, 1 bay leaf, tied)
- 1 garlic clove
- 1 tablespoon sea salt
- 1 teaspoon black peppercorns
- 1.3l water, cold
- 200ml white wine, boiled for 2 minutes

**For the Spinach and Watercress Purée**
- 1 tablespoon olive oil
- 200g baby spinach, washed, drained and roughly chopped
- 320g watercress, washed, drained and roughly chopped
- 2 pinches of sea salt
- pinch of black pepper, freshly ground
- 50ml soya cream

**For the Lemon Sabayon**
- 3 egg yolks, medium
- 4 tablespoons cold water
- 2 tablespoons olive oil
- pinch of sea salt
- pinch of cayenne pepper
- 1 dessertspoon lemon juice

In a large saucepan on a high heat add all the ingredients for the stock. Boil, skim, reduce the heat and simmer for 20 minutes.

To make the purée, heat the oil in a large pan on a medium heat and add the spinach and watercress. Season with the salt and pepper and cook for 3 minutes with a lid on. Add the cream, bring to a boil and simmer for a further minute. Pour the mixture into a food processor and pulse for about 10 seconds until a rough texture is achieved. Taste and adjust the seasoning if required. Place in a hot serving dish and cover until required.

To cook the lemon sabayon fill a large saucepan one-third full with water and bring to the boil. Set a large stainless steel bowl on top of the saucepan, place the egg yolks and water in the bowl and whisk vigorously for about 5 minutes until you obtain a light and lemon-coloured foam, about 6 or 7 times its original volume. Continue whisking until the foam has more texture but is still thin enough to run.

Pour the olive oil into the sabayon, whisk briefly. Season with salt, cayenne pepper and lemon juice. Taste and adjust the seasoning if necessary.

To cook the salmon steaks slide them into the simmering stock. Bring the pan back to a gentle simmer and cook the fish for 5 minutes. Turn off the heat and leave the salmon for a further 2–3 minutes.

To serve, spoon the spinach and watercress purée into the middle of your plates, add the poached salmon and some of the poached vegetables on top and generously spoon the sauce on and around the fish.

*Good source of* **Allium** *vegetables, cruciferous vegetables, oily fish, selenium and vitamin D. Source of vitamin E*
PER PORTION: 549 KCAL, 37.1G FAT, 6.6G SATURATED FAT

# saag aloo with oily fish

This dish was kindly provided by TV chef and restaurateur Cyrus Todiwala. Here is what he has to say about it:

*'This dish can be prepared with deep-fried potatoes in place of the boiled ones. Simply blanch the potatoes first, deep-fry until golden, drain well and add at the very end. Fenugreek gives a very good flavour to this dish. It is available in packets and is known as "kasoori methi". It needs to be placed in a tray in a very slow oven until it develops a beautiful aroma. It is then crushed and sieved for tiny twigs etc., and used in its powdered form, to flavour spinach and other dishes. To provide extra selenium, you can replace the oily fish with prawns or diced liver and kidney. They work extremely well with this too and can be stirred into the Saag Aloo before serving.'*

SERVES 6–8

**For the Saag Aloo**
- 750g baby potatoes or ordinary ones, cubed
- 10–12 bunches of fresh spinach or 1kg picked leaves or chopped frozen spinach
- 3 tablespoons rapeseed oil
- 10g cumin seeds
- 2 dried red chillies, broken into pieces
- 20g fresh ginger, chopped
- 20g garlic, finely chopped
- salt and crushed black pepper
- dried fenugreek, optional for taste
- 1 large tablespoon fresh coriander, chopped

**For the Fish**
- 100–150g oily fish per person – fresh sardines, mackerel, tuna or swordfish will all work well
- ground turmeric, about 1 teaspoon for every 300g fish
- lime juice, 1 lime for every 300g fish
- a little rapeseed oil for cooking

Boil the potatoes until soft but still firm. Blanch the spinach briefly in boiling water, taking care not to overcook it; drain and either finely chop or purée. If puréeing the spinach, there may be no need to blanch in water as the spinach will contain a great deal of water and will wilt down in a dry saucepan.

Heat the oil in a deep pan or a frying pan large enough to hold all the potato and the spinach – a wok would be ideal. Add the cumin and red chilli pieces and cook for about half a minute or so. Add the chopped ginger and garlic and continue cooking.

As the garlic begins to turn a deep golden colour add the spinach and sauté for a few minutes stirring regularly. Add salt and crushed pepper to taste and dried crumbled fenugreek if you are using it. Stir in the potatoes and simmer for a minute or two until they are heated through. Stir in the fresh chopped coriander for the final touch.

Meanwhile, to prepare the fish, marinate in the turmeric and lime juice. Brush the fish with a little oil and cook under the grill or in a frying pan on the hob for a few minutes until the flesh flakes. Slice the fish and place on to the Saag Aloo to serve.

*Good source of oily fish and vitamin D. Source of Allium vegetables, selenium and vitamin E.*
PER PORTION: 393 KCAL, 20.6G FAT, 3.4G SATURATED FAT

# POM stuffed halibut

This fish dish can be served with rice and fresh green vegetables such as peas or beans. Other fish can be used – just make sure that the fillets are thin enough to roll. This dish has been adapted from a recipe on www.pomwonderful.com.

SERVES 4

- 580g halibut fillets, 1.5cm thick
- 1 teaspoon salt
- 3 tablespoons olive oil
- 1 onion, thinly sliced
- 3 garlic cloves, crushed
- ¼ teaspoon freshly ground black pepper
- 30g chopped walnuts
- 1 tablespoon slivered candied orange peel

- 240ml pomegranate juice
- ¼ teaspoon ground saffron, dissolved in 2 tablespoons hot water
- 2 tablespoons fresh lime juice

**For the Garnish**
- 2 tablespoons chopped walnuts
- 2 tablespoons pomegranate arils

Preheat the oven to 200°C/400°F/gas 6.

Rinse the fish in cold water, pat dry with kitchen paper and rub both sides with salt and set aside. Heat 2 tablespoons of oil in a large frying pan and brown the onion and garlic.

Add the pepper, walnuts, candied peel and pomegranate juice and cook for 3 minutes. Mix well and remove from the heat.

Lay the fish out on a baking dish and place a quarter of the stuffing on one end of each of the fish fillets. Gently roll the fish from the stuffing end and pin closed with a cocktail stick if necessary. Pour the saffron water, the remaining oil and the lime juice over the fish.

Place in the oven and bake for 10–15 minutes, basting from time to time, until the fish flakes easily with a fork. Arrange the fish on a serving platter. Pour the sauce from the baking dish over the fish and garnish with walnuts and pomegranate arils.

*Good source of Allium vegetables and selenium. Source of polyphenols and vitamin E*
PER PORTION: 454 KCAL, 27.2G FAT, 3.1G SATURATED FAT

# liver and onions

This rich and traditional meal is great comfort food served on a mound of mashed potato. This recipe has been selected from *Cooking with the Kosher Butcher's Wife* by Sharon Lurie.

SERVES 4–5

- 500g calf's or ox's liver, sliced
- 75g plain flour
- 3 large onions, halved and sliced into half rounds
- little olive oil for frying
- ½ teaspoon freshly crushed garlic

- 55ml red wine (optional)
- 225ml chicken stock (either home-made or 1 chicken stock cube dissolved in 225ml hot water)
- freshly ground black pepper (optional)

Cut the liver into the desired size and coat with the flour. Fry the onions in oil until glassy, then add the garlic and toss for a minute or two.

Add the liver to the onions and continue frying on medium heat or until the onions are golden brown. Don't allow the pan to burn as this will give the gravy a bitter taste.

Add the wine, if using, and add the chicken stock, stirring as you do so to get all the bits off the bottom of the pan. This, together with the onions, gives the gravy its delicious taste. Leave the gravy to thicken and reduce slightly.

If you feel your gravy is too thick, add a little more water and bring to the boil. Add salt and freshly ground black pepper.

**Good source of Allium *vegetables and selenium***
PER PORTION: 331 KCAL, 11.6G FAT, 2.2G SATURATED FAT

# moroccan lamb stew

This is a fragrant stew with a Moroccan vibe. Don't let the number of ingredients put you off – the oven does the hard work!

SERVES 6

- 3 tablespoons olive oil
- 1 large onion, finely chopped
- 1 tablespoon ground cumin
- 1 tablespoon ground cinnamon
- 1 dessertspoon turmeric
- black pepper
- 5 garlic cloves, finely chopped
- 700g lamb, trimmed of fat and chopped into 2cm cubes
- 2 x 400g tins chopped tomatoes
- 3 tablespoons tomato purée
- 200g carrots, chopped into batons
- 400g parsnips, chopped into batons

- 75g dried apricots, roughly chopped
- 75g sultanas
- 600ml lamb or chicken stock
- 400g tin chickpeas
- small bunch of fresh coriander, chopped
- 150g low-fat yogurt or soya yogurt

*For the Couscous*
- 375g couscous
- 1 tablespoon mint sauce or chopped, fresh mint
- 100g pomegranate arils

Preheat the oven to 150°C/300°F/gas 2.

Heat 2 tablespoons of the oil in a large casserole dish and gently cook the onion and spices for 10 minutes, adding the garlic for the last 3 minutes.

Meanwhile, in a separate pan, cook the lamb in the remaining oil for 8 minutes. Add the lamb to the casserole dish and stir in the chopped tomatoes, tomato purée, chopped vegetables, dried fruits and stock. Bring to the boil, cover and put in the oven for 2 hours.

Stir in the chickpeas for the second hour and 10 minutes before the stew is ready, stir the mint into the couscous and cook according to packet instructions. When the couscous is ready, fluff it up with a fork and stir in the pomegranate arils. Serve the stew and couscous with a little yogurt and the chopped coriander sprinkled on top.

**Good source of Allium *vegetables and lycopene. Source of legumes and vitamin E***
PER PORTION: 619 KCAL, 20.1G FAT, 5.8G SATURATED FAT

# beef and lentil cottage pie

This provides a hearty meal full of flavour. Using lentils gives the benefit of legumes while reducing the quantity of red meat. Serve on its own or with vegetables.

SERVES 4

- 250g lean minced beef
- 1 large onion
- 150g green lentils, rinsed
- 400g tin chopped tomatoes
- 4 carrots, peeled and diced
- 150g frozen peas
- 200ml beef or vegetable stock
- 2 tablespoons tomato ketchup

**For the Mash**
- 1kg potatoes, peeled and chopped
- 25g olive spread
- 2–3 tablespoons milk or soya milk

Preheat the oven to 180°C/350°F/gas 4.

Put the mince and onions in a large saucepan and cook until the mince has browned. Add the remaining ingredients and cook for about 30 minutes until the lentils and vegetables are soft, adding a little water if necessary. Pour into an ovenproof dish.

Meanwhile boil the potatoes until tender. Drain and mash them, adding the olive spread and enough milk to make a soft mash. Scoop the mash on top of the mince mixture and place in the oven for 30 minutes or until the top is golden brown.

**Good source of selenium. Source of Allium vegetables, lycopene and legumes**
PER PORTION: 541 KCAL, 11.8G FAT, 3.2G SATURATED FAT

# small meats (laham saghir)

This recipe was picked up by Granny Dilley during her years in Yemen and she doubts there is a formal recipe for it. It owes a lot to the old trading contacts between Yemen, Indonesia and India. It is traditional to add a fair whack of finely chopped garlic lightly stirred in or sprinkled on top just before serving – but you can add it all at the beginning. Serve with French bread or rice and 'Chop-it-up' (page 147). This recipe has been kindly provided by Mrs John Dilley.

SERVES 2

- 1 tablespoon soya oil
- 1 medium onion, fairly finely chopped
- 3–4 garlic cloves, finely chopped
- 1 dessertspoon curry powder or paste (Hot Madras)
- 1 dessertspoon ground cumin
- 1 chilli (Thai bird's eye), chopped with seeds (or more to taste)
- 1 dessertspoon ground coriander
- 1 small–medium waxy potato, diced into 1cm cubes (optional)
- 225g lamb's liver and/or kidneys, coarsely diced
- 1 tablespoon tomato purée
- 400g tin chopped tomatoes
- sea salt and ground black pepper

Heat the oil in a frying pan over a medium heat and lightly fry the onion, garlic, spices, chilli and potato (if using) for about 10 minutes. Stir occasionally and do not allow to burn; add a little extra oil if necessary.

Add the 'small meats', tomato purée and chopped tomatoes, swirl a little water around the inside of the tin and pour into the pan. Season with salt and pepper. Cook on a medium–high heat for 5–10 minutes or until cooked through and the sauce has the degree of thickness you like, stirring occasionally. Serve hot or cold. This dish improves with keeping and can be made a day in advance.

*Good source of* **Allium** *vegetables, lycopene and selenium. Source of vitamin E*
PER PORTION: 332 KCAL, 14.2G FAT, 2.5G SATURATED FAT

# dr john's meatballs

This is a satisfying dish of succulent meatballs in a deliciously rich sauce. To reduce the amount of meat, simply replace 250g minced steak with 250g tofu that has been mashed with a fork and crumble in two beef stock cubes. Small new potatoes can be added to the casserole for the last 30–40 minutes of cooking.

SERVES 4

- 1kg onions
- 2 tablespoons olive oil
- 1 dessertspoon cornflour
- salt and pepper

**For the Meatballs**
- 500g minced steak
- 1 medium egg, beaten
- 1 teaspoon horseradish sauce, or more to taste
- salt and pepper
- 1 tablespoon plain flour
- 1 tablespoon olive oil

Preheat the oven to 180°C/350°F/gas 4.

Finely slice the onions and sweat gently in the olive oil in an iron casserole until they are a uniform mid- to dark brown. Mix the cornflour with a little cold water in a jug and then add boiling water to the mixture to make up to 600ml. Add the cornflour and water mixture to the onions and stir. Add a good amount of salt and pepper and simmer very gently until you are ready to add the meatballs.

In a large bowl combine the meat, beaten egg and horseradish sauce and a good seasoning of salt and pepper. Add sufficient flour to bind the mixture (about a tablespoon). Form the meat mixture into small balls about the size of a golf ball.

Fry gently in a frying pan in 1 tablespoon of olive oil, until they are browned all over. Remove from the pan and drain on kitchen paper. Put the meatballs into the simmering sauce, cover tightly and cook in a moderate oven for 1½ hours or until the meatballs are tender, adding a little more water if necessary. Adjust seasoning before serving.

*Good source of Allium vegetables. Source of selenium*
PER PORTION: 479 KCAL, 29.0G FAT, 10.3G SATURATED FAT

# stir-fried pork fillet

There are numerous ways you could vary this tasty stir-fry: you could use chicken breast instead of pork, add a tablespoon of fish sauce in with the soy sauce, or add peanuts or cashew nuts. Why not try some of the following as alternative or additional vegetables: courgettes, mangetout, tinned water chestnuts, tinned bamboo shoots or mushrooms.

SERVES 4

**For the Pork and Marinade**
- 2 tablespoons soy sauce, plus extra to taste
- 1 tablespoon lemon juice
- 1 teaspoon brown sugar
- 1 pork fillet, cut into thin strips

**For the Vegetable Stir-fry**
- 2 tablespoons rapeseed oil
- 2.5cm fresh ginger, grated
- 2 garlic cloves, chopped

- 1 red chilli, deseeded and chopped
- 1 red onion, thinly sliced
- 1 head of broccoli, broken into small florets
- 1 pak choi, sliced
- 1 bunch of spring onions, chopped into 1.5cm pieces
- 320g bean sprouts
- 1 each of red, green and yellow peppers, sliced into thin strips
- salt

Combine the marinade ingredients in a bowl and add the pork strips. Leave in the fridge to marinate for at least 2 hours, or ideally overnight.

Drain the meat from the marinade and pat dry with kitchen paper. Heat the oil in a large wok. When the oil is just smoking, stir-fry the ginger, garlic and chilli for 10–20 seconds and then add the pork. Stir-fry the pork until lightly browned, add the red onion and broccoli and stir-fry for a further minute. Add the remaining vegetables and continue to stir-fry for a further 4–5 minutes.

Add the marinade from the meat and a little more soy sauce to taste and cook for a further 2 minutes. Season with salt and serve with boiled rice.

*Good source of Allium vegetables, cruciferous vegetables and legumes*
PER PORTION: 223 KCAL, 9.9G FAT, 1.3G SATURATED FAT

# badak chaanti badami pasanda (stuffed duck breast in a creamy sauce)

This dish has been kindly provided by TV chef and restaurateur Cyrus Todiwala. This is what he has to say about it:

> *'The sauce is a version of korma and can be used with any other meat, fish, poultry or vegetables. The word* pasanda *represents the stuffing and relates to any form of stuffing.* Badami *stands for "with or of almonds".'*

This recipe requires ginger and garlic paste which is very easy to make. Simply blend together equal quantities of garlic and fresh ginger with a little oil and water until a smooth purée is formed.

This paste can be kept in the fridge for up to six months in an airtight jar.

SERVES 6

- 6 medium-sized duck breasts

**For the Stuffing**
- 150g ricotta or paneer
- 6–8 whole almonds, sliced or coarsely chopped
- 6–8 Brazil nuts, sliced or coarsely chopped, plus extra to garnish
- 10–15 sultanas
- generous pinch of cardamom powder
- salt to taste
- 1 tablespoon chopped fresh coriander
- a few threads saffron (a small pinch will give you the desired number of threads)

**For the Sauce**
- 2 tablespoons rapeseed oil
- 2 medium onions, sliced
- 1 tablespoon ginger and garlic paste
- ¼ teaspoon turmeric powder
- ½ teaspoon cumin powder
- ¾ teaspoon coriander powder
- ½ teaspoon chilli powder
- 100g ground almonds
- 100g cashew nuts

**For the Tempering**
- 1 tablespoon rapeseed oil
- 2.5cm piece cinnamon
- 3–4 cardamom pods
- 3 cloves
- 2 peppercorns
- 1 mace flower broken into two
- 1–2 bay leaves

Blend all the stuffing ingredients together, season to taste and set aside in the refrigerator to keep firm.

Trim some of the skin and fat from the duck breasts but do not remove it all. With a thin, sharp knife, slit the duck breasts through the middle and carefully open them out, taking care not to pierce the meat or separate it completely. With gentle, short strokes the meat should separate fairly easily and cleanly. Open the duck breasts out and lay them out in a row.

Spoon equal quantities of the stuffing on to one edge of each of the open duck breasts, fold the edge over the stuffing and roll up until you have a sausage. Once rolled, wrap each duck breast in a piece of aluminium foil or greaseproof paper. Place them in a large pan or iron casserole deep enough to fit them all. Pour over enough hot or boiling water to cover and simmer for about 20 minutes. Leave the duck breasts to cool in the liquid. When cold, skim off any fat and retain the stock for the sauce.

To cook the sauce, heat the oil in a large pan or iron casserole. Add the onions and sauté for 5–6 minutes or until opaque. Add the ginger and garlic paste and all the spices and sauté for 2–3 minutes. Next add the ground almonds and cashews and sauté for 4–5 minutes, stirring with a wooden spatula but do not allow to burn. Add about 250ml of the reserved stock and stir. If the mixture gets too thick, add some more. Boil gently for 15 minutes or until the onions and cashew nuts are cooked. If the sauce thickens too much add a little more stock. Cool the sauce and purée in the blender. Reheat the sauce and bring to a slow boil stirring regularly.

Heat the oil for the tempering and fry the spices. When they are browned and swollen put them into the sauce, stir well and season to taste. To serve, remove the duck breasts from the foil, clean the sides with kitchen paper and place them in the hot sauce. Continue to heat the sauce very gently until the duck breasts are thoroughly reheated. Slice the duck breasts and serve on a platter with the sauce poured on top. Garnish with some extra slivers of Brazil nuts.

*Good source of* **Allium** *vegetables and selenium. Source of vitamin E*
PER PORTION: 584 KCAL, 39.2G FAT, 7.6G SATURATED FAT

# stuffed aubergine (karniyarik)

These aubergines stuffed with minced meat are served as a hot main dish with rice pilaf. Use small, elongated aubergines (at most 14cm long), weighing about 125g. This dish has been selected from *Arabesque* by Claudia Roden.

SERVES 6

- 6 thin and long medium-sized aubergines
- 1 tablespoon salt
- 2–3 tablespoons sunflower oil
- 2 onions, chopped
- 400g minced beef or lamb
- 1 tablespoon tomato paste
- 2 large tomatoes, peeled and chopped
- 1 teaspoon ground cinnamon
- ½ teaspoon ground allspice
- black pepper
- large bunch of flat-leaf parsley, chopped
- 250ml tomato juice

Preheat the oven to 180°C/350°F/gas 4.

Trim the caps but leave the stems on the aubergines. Peel 1.25cm strips off the skins lengthways, leaving 1.25cm strips of peel. Soak the aubergines in water mixed with 1 tablespoon of salt for 30 minutes, then drain and dry. Fry 2–3 at a time very briefly in hot shallow oil, turning to brown them lightly all over. Drain on kitchen paper.

For the filling, fry the onions in another pan in 2–3 tablespoons oil until soft. Add the meat and cook for about 10 minutes. Add the tomato paste and one of the tomatoes, spice, salt and pepper. Stir well and simmer until the liquid is reduced.

Place the aubergines side by side in a single layer in an ovenproof dish. With a sharp pointed knife, make a slit in each one, lengthways, along one of the bare strips on the top until about 2.5cm from each end. Carefully open the slits and, with a dessertspoon, press against the flesh on the insides to make a hollow pocket. Fill each of the aubergines with the filling, and place a slice of the remaining tomato on top. Pour the tomato juice into the dish, cover with foil, and bake in the oven for about 40 minutes or until the aubergines are soft.

*Good source of lycopene. Source of* **Allium** *vegetables and vitamin E*
PER PORTION: 265 KCAL, 16.5G FAT, 5.6G SATURATED FAT

# chicken cobbler

This chicken cobbler makes a hearty mid-week meal. You could substitute 300ml of the chicken stock with white wine if preferred.

SERVES 4

- 500g skinless chicken breast, diced
- 1 tablespoon plain flour
- 2 tablespoons rapeseed oil
- 2 medium leeks, sliced
- 300g frozen broad beans
- 300g carrots, peeled and sliced or diced
- 2 celery sticks, sliced
- 600ml chicken stock

**For the Scone Topping**
- 225g self-raising flour
- 1 teaspoon baking powder
- ½ teaspoon salt
- 25g olive spread
- 1 tablespoon sunflower seed kernels
- 1 egg, beaten
- water to mix

Preheat the oven to 180°C/350°F/gas 4.

Toss the diced chicken breast in the flour until it is coated. Heat the oil in an iron casserole, add the chicken pieces and cook, stirring until the meat has sealed. Add the vegetables and cook, stirring for a further 2–3 minutes. Add the stock and bring to the boil. Cover the casserole and put it in the oven for about 1 hour.

Check the casserole towards the end of the cooking time and add some water if necessary. Meanwhile make the scone topping. Sift the flour and baking powder into a bowl and add the salt. Rub in the olive spread until the mixture resembles fine breadcrumbs. Stir in the sunflower seeds and then the egg and about 2–3 tablespoons of water to form a soft dough. Divide the mixture into 8 equal portions and roll into balls.

When the casserole has cooked for an hour, remove it from the oven and place the scone balls on top. Brush the scones with any remaining beaten egg or a little milk. Return the casserole, uncovered, to the oven for 20–30 minutes or until the scones are golden brown.

*Source of Allium vegetables, legumes, selenium and vitamin E*
PER PORTION: 548 KCAL, 14.9G FAT, 2.5G SATURATED FAT

# chicken kebabs with peanut sauce

You can substitute the chicken with pork fillet or beef fillet. Serve with plain boiled rice and Broccoli Daltali (page 153). The peanut sauce will freeze very well. This recipe has been kindly provided by Dr John Rayman.

SERVES 4

- 4 chicken breasts, sliced into thick strips

**For the Marinade**
- 3 tablespoons soy sauce
- 1 tablespoon lemon juice
- 1 tablespoon olive oil
- 1 medium onion, chopped
- 3 garlic cloves, chopped
- 1 teaspoon chilli powder
- 2.5cm piece fresh ginger, grated
- 2 teaspoons brown sugar

**For the Peanut Sauce**
- ½ teaspoon turmeric
- ½ teaspoon curry powder
- ½ teaspoon cayenne pepper
- 2 teaspoons sugar
- 250ml coconut milk
- 100g salted peanuts, coarsely ground
- 1 teaspoon lemon juice, or to taste
- salt

Mix all the marinade ingredients together in a bowl and add the chicken, ensuring that all the pieces are covered. Leave to marinate in the fridge for 24 hours.

Preheat the oven to 200°C/400°F/gas 6.

To make the sauce add the turmeric, curry powder, cayenne pepper and sugar to the coconut milk and bring gently to the boil. Stirring constantly, add the peanuts and simmer for 2–3 minutes or until the sauce has thickened. Add lemon juice and salt to taste. You may need to add a little more coconut milk if the sauce becomes too thick.

Thread the strips of chicken concertina-fashion on to metal skewers and place on a baking tray. Cook in the oven for 25–30 minutes or until the chicken is cooked through, basting with the marinade occasionally. Serve with the peanut sauce.

*Good source of Allium vegetables. Source of selenium, legumes*
PER PORTION: 476 KCAL, 20.6G FAT, 4.0G SATURATED FAT

# thai green curry

This is a fragrant, oriental curry which can be served in bowls with rice and soy sauce. This recipe has been kindly provided by Sarah Dilley.

SERVES 4

- 1 tablespoon flavourless oil or nut oil
- 4 tablespoons Thai green curry paste
- 4 chicken breasts, cubed
- 1 carrot, sliced into rounds
- 1 pepper, sliced
- 160g frozen soya beans
- 40g green beans
- 360g broccoli
- 400g tin coconut milk
- 1 tablespoon fish sauce
- small bunch of fresh coriander, chopped
- lime wedges to serve

Heat the oil in a wok or large frying pan over a medium–high heat. Add the Thai green curry paste and cook, stirring, for 2 minutes.

Add the chicken breasts and stir-fry for 5 minutes, then add all the vegetables to the pan and stir-fry for a further 3 minutes.

Pour in the coconut milk and fish sauce and leave to simmer for 5–10 minutes, stirring occasionally, until the vegetables are cooked and the sauce has thickened. Stir in most of the chopped coriander. Garnish with lime wedges and the remaining coriander to serve.

*Good source of cruciferous vegetables. Source of selenium and soya*
PER PORTION: 433 KCAL, 13.2G FAT, 3.1G SATURATED FAT

# persian rice with chicken and tomatoes

This colourful, family-pleasing dish is based on a Persian recipe. The amounts and combinations of spices can be altered according to what you have in the cupboard. You could use pork or lamb in place of the chicken and serve with a leafy salad.

SERVES 6

- 1 teaspoon turmeric
- ½ teaspoon cardamom pods
- ½ teaspoon cumin
- ½ teaspoon cinnamon
- ½ teaspoon coriander seeds
- pinch of caraway seeds
- 4 peppercorns
- 6 cloves
- 1 tablespoon olive oil
- 1 large onion, sliced
- 4 garlic cloves, finely chopped
- salt
- 560g chicken (4 breast fillets), cut into small cubes
- 3 tablespoons tomato purée
- 350g long-grain rice (basmati)
- 180g new potatoes (or any waxy potatoes, e.g. Maris Piper), chopped into small cubes
- 500g cherry tomatoes or 400g tin chopped tomatoes
- fresh coriander, chopped, to serve
- yogurt or soya yogurt, to serve (optional)

Grind together the spices with a pestle and mortar. Heat the oil and lightly fry the onion in a large saucepan for about 5 minutes. Add the garlic and continue to fry until the onion is soft and golden.

Stir in the spices and salt and cook for a minute. Add the chicken and fry, stirring, for about 8 minutes until browned. Stir in the tomato purée, then the rice and potatoes, then the tomatoes.

Add 800ml boiling water, cover and simmer on a low heat for 30 minutes until the rice is cooked and has absorbed all the water. To serve, top with a little yogurt and sprinkle with fresh coriander.

*Good source of Allium vegetables. Source of lycopene, selenium*
PER PORTION: 430 KCAL, 5.2G FAT, 1.0G SATURATED FAT

# chicken with walnut and pomegranate sauce

This delicious dish should be eaten with plain rice and a green salad. The recipe has been kindly provided by Dr John Rayman.

SERVES 4

- 3 tablespoons olive oil
- 1 large onion, finely chopped
- 100g walnuts, coarsely chopped, plus extra to garnish
- juice of 2 oranges
- 400ml pomegranate juice
- 1 teaspoon salt
- 1 teaspoon cinnamon
- 1 tablespoon sugar
- ¼ tablespoon saffron
- 50g flour
- 1 teaspoon turmeric
- 1 medium chicken, skinned and jointed
- handful of pomegranate arils to serve (optional)

Fry the onion gently in 1 tablespoon of olive oil in a heavy-based casserole until light brown in colour. Add the walnuts and cook very slowly for 4 minutes, stirring continuously to prevent the mixture from burning.

Add the orange juice, pomegranate juice, salt, cinnamon, sugar and saffron. Simmer on a low heat for 2–3 minutes. Mix the flour and turmeric on a flat plate. Carefully roll each chicken piece in the mixture to cover thoroughly.

Heat 2 tablespoons of olive oil in a large frying pan and fry the chicken over a low–medium heat until it is golden brown all over. Remove from the pan and drain on kitchen paper.

Add the chicken pieces to the walnut and pomegranate sauce and simmer for 40 minutes or until the chicken is tender and thoroughly cooked. Garnish with walnut halves and pomegranate arils, if desired.

*Good source of polyphenols. Source of* Allium *vegetables and selenium*
PER PORTION: 614 KCAL, 31.2G FAT, 4.0G SATURATED FAT

# pheasant with sun-dried shiitake mushrooms

This dish is excellent served with peas or snow peas and boiled new potatoes. It can also be made with other kinds of game such as partridge. For an additional source of selenium, if you have the livers of the pheasants, they can be added at the end of the browning stage. This dish has been kindly provided by Dr John Rayman.

SERVES 6

- 300g sun-dried shiitake mushrooms
- 3 tablespoons olive oil
- 2 pheasants, cleaned and dried
- 400ml good red wine
- 1 tablespoon flour
- 20 button onions

Preheat the oven to 200°C/400°F/gas 6.

Soak the mushrooms in warm water according to the packet instructions, drain and reserve for later. Heat 2 tablespoons of olive oil in a heavy-bottomed frying pan and cook the pheasants until fairly tender and nicely browned all over.

Remove to a heavy casserole and keep warm. Add red wine to the frying pan and bring to the boil. Reduce to half the volume, stir in the flour and pour over the reserved birds. Season with salt and pepper. Blanch the onions in boiling salted water and dry. Heat 1 tablespoon of olive oil in a frying pan, brown the onions and add to the casserole.

Put the casserole in the oven and cook for 45 minutes or until the birds are tender. Towards the end of the cooking add the mushrooms to the casserole. Adjust the seasoning and serve.

*Good source of* **Allium** *vegetables and vitamin D. Source of selenium*
PER PORTION: 502 KCAL, 12.9G FAT, 2.7G SATURATED FAT

# jardaloo ma murghi (chicken with apricots)

This dish has been kindly provided by TV chef and restaurateur Cyrus Todiwala. This is what he has to say about it:

*'This is a very popular Parsee chicken preparation served at festive occasions and dates back to our Persian ancestry. This dish can be served garnished with crispy straw potatoes and accompanied with chapattis, bread or plain rice.'*

SERVES 4–6

- 200g dried apricots
- 4 tablespoons rapeseed oil
- 2 x 2.5cm pieces cinnamon stick
- 2 medium onions, chopped
- 2 heaped tablespoons ginger and garlic paste (see note on recipe page 116)
- 500–600g chicken, cut into 2cm dice
- 400g tin chopped tomatoes
- salt to taste
- 1–2 tablespoons coriander, chopped

**For the Masala**
- 6–8 large sized dry red chillis
- 1½ teaspoons cumin seeds
- 1½ tablespoons coriander seeds
- 2.5cm piece cinnamon stick
- 4–5 green cardamom pods
- 4–5 cloves

Soak the apricots in advance in about 250ml of warm water for 2–3 hours or overnight, until they are swollen and soft. Grind the masala spices together with as little water as possible to make a thick paste and set aside.

Heat the oil in a thick-bottomed pan until hazy and add the cinnamon sticks. After about 1½ minutes, add the onions and brown slowly. Add the masala and ginger and garlic paste, and sauté well until the absorbed oil is released slowly around the edges of the combined masala and onions. Add the chicken and sauté for 4–5 minutes.

Salt to taste and add the chopped tomatoes and the apricots along with any water that has not been absorbed. Mix well, cover and simmer until the chicken is cooked through. If the gravy becomes too thin, remove the lid. Blend in the chopped coriander, check the seasoning and serve.

***Good source of Allium vegetables. Source of lycopene, selenium and vitamin E***
PER PORTION: 409 KCAL, 17.3G FAT, 1.2G SATURATED FAT

# turkey and apricot bake

This creamy recipe is simple to make and a real family pleaser. Using soya milk rather than regular milk not only reduces the dairy but increases the soya content. To make this dish dairy-free, simply replace the cheese with a cheese substitute. This dish has been adapted from a Sainsbury's recipe.

SERVES 4

- 450g turkey, cut into strips
- 25g plain flour
- ground black pepper
- 1 tablespoon olive oil
- 80g spring onions, sliced
- 150g dried apricots, chopped
- 300ml soya milk
- 75g mature Cheddar cheese, grated

**For the Topping**
- 40g wholemeal breadcrumbs
- 25g Brazil nuts, chopped
- 2 tablespoons fresh parsley, chopped
- 25g mature Cheddar cheese, grated

Preheat the oven to 190°C/375°F/gas 5.

Coat the turkey strips in the flour, seasoned with pepper. Heat the oil in a non-stick saucepan. Add the turkey and cook for 2–3 minutes, stirring continually until sealed.

Stir in the spring onions and apricots, followed by the soya milk. Cook for 2–3 minutes, stirring until thickened and smooth. Stir in 75g of the cheese and transfer the mixture to an ovenproof dish. Mix together the breadcrumbs, nuts, most of the parsley and the cheese. Sprinkle this over the turkey mixture.

Bake for 15 minutes. For a crispy topping, place under a preheated grill for 1–2 minutes. Garnish with the remaining parsley.

***Good source of selenium. Source of Allium vegetables and soya***
PER PORTION: 435 KCAL, 19.2G FAT, 7.6G SATURATED FAT

# sweet and sour turkey meatballs

Serve these tasty meatballs with mashed potatoes and fresh vegetables. This dish has been adapted from a recipe in *Body and Beauty Foods* by Hazel Courteney and Kathryn Marsden.

SERVES 4

- 450g turkey mince
- 4 shallots or 1 onion, finely chopped
- 2 garlic cloves, crushed
- 115g mushrooms, finely chopped
- 2 teaspoons mixed dried herbs
- 55g fresh wholemeal breadcrumbs
- 2 tablespoons tomato purée
- salt and pepper
- a little wholemeal flour
- 1 tablespoon olive oil

*For the Sauce*
- 1 tablespoon cornflour
- 4 tablespoons red wine
- 400g tin chopped tomatoes, puréed
- 150ml unsweetened apple juice
- 2 tablespoons red wine vinegar
- 2 tablespoons brown sugar
- 1 tablespoon tomato purée

Preheat the oven to 180°C/350°F/gas 4.

Put all the meatball ingredients, except the flour and the oil, in a bowl and mix well. Roll the mixture into small balls. Sprinkle the flour on to a plate and roll each meatball lightly in it. Place the meatballs on a plate and chill for 20 minutes.

To make the sauce, blend the cornflour with the red wine and put into a saucepan. Add the remaining sauce ingredients. Bring to the boil, stirring continuously, then reduce the heat and simmer while cooking the meatballs.

Heat the oil in a frying pan and fry the meatballs over a medium heat for 5–10 minutes, until light brown. Transfer to an ovenproof dish and pour the sauce over the meatballs. Cover and bake for about 45 minutes or until the meatballs are cooked.

**Source of Allium *vegetables, lycopene and selenium***
PER PORTION: 293 KCAL, 5.5G FAT, 1.0G SATURATED FAT

# falafel with tomato and cucumber relish

Falafel is a popular street food in many countries around the world. By baking it rather than deep-frying the fat content is instantly reduced. This vegetarian classic tastes great with the tomato and cucumber relish.

SERVES 6

- 6 wholemeal pitta breads
- 60g salad leaves

*For the Falafel*
- 2 x 400g tins chickpeas, drained
- 3 garlic cloves, peeled
- 1 large onion, chopped
- 1 teaspoon ground cumin
- ½ teaspoon ground coriander
- pinch of cayenne pepper or 1 teaspoon chilli powder

- salt and pepper
- 20g fresh parsley, chopped
- 2 tablespoons lemon juice
- 1 tablespoon olive oil

*For the Tomato and Cucumber Relish*
- 3 tomatoes
- ½ cucumber
- 150ml soya yogurt
- 1 tablespoon mint sauce

Preheat the oven to 180°C/350°F/gas 4.

Put all the falafel ingredients except the olive oil in a food-processor and whizz until coarse; do not allow the mixture to become smooth. If you have time, make the mixture in advance and chill in the fridge for a few hours to allow the flavours to infuse. Form small handfuls of the mixture into 12–16 balls. Wearing plastic gloves makes the falafel easier to handle as they stop it sticking to your hands.

Grease a baking tray with the olive oil and place the falafel balls on it. Bake in the oven for 30 minutes or until golden brown, turning once. To make the relish, chop the tomatoes and cucumber into small cubes of uniform size. In a bowl, mix the tomato and cucumber with the soya yogurt and mint. Warm the pitta breads in the oven for a few minutes, not allowing them to go crispy. Serve the falafel with the pitta bread, soya yogurt relish and salad leaves.

**Good source of Allium *vegetables and legumes. Source of soya and vitamin E***
PER PORTION: 304 KCAL, 6.9G FAT, 0.9G SATURATED FAT

# spicy bean pitta

These spicy bean pittas make a filling and warming lunch. This dish has been adapted from a recipe in Morrisons' *Let's Eat Smart* magazine.

SERVES 4

- 2 tablespoons olive oil
- 8 spring onions, finely chopped
- 1 red pepper, diced
- 400g tin butter beans, drained and rinsed
- 400g tin chopped tomatoes
- 2 tablespoons sweet chilli sauce
- 4 wholemeal pitta breads
- 1 bunch of watercress

Heat the oil in a small pan. Add the spring onions and red pepper and sauté until tender.

Add the butter beans, tomatoes and chilli sauce and cook until the sauce thickens. Slice the pitta breads in half and lightly toast if preferred.

Spoon the butter bean mixture into the pitta breads and garnish with the watercress.

***Source of** Allium **vegetables, cruciferous vegetables, legumes, lycopene and vitamin E***
PER PORTION: 407 KCAL, 9.0G FAT, 1.4G SATURATED FAT

# bean burgers

Make these bean burgers as spicy or mild as you like by simply adding more or less chilli. Serve them in a burger bun with ketchup and a side salad.

SERVES 4

- 1 medium potato, peeled and chopped
- 2 tablespoons oil
- 1 medium onion, finely chopped
- 3 garlic cloves, finely chopped
- 1 teaspoon cumin
- 1 teaspoon coriander
- 1 red chilli or 1 teaspoon chilli powder or to taste
- 240g frozen soya beans
- 400g tin kidney beans, drained
- small bunch of fresh coriander
- salt and pepper
- 4 tablespoons sweetcorn

Boil the potato in a pan of boiling water for 15 minutes or until soft; drain and mash. Heat a tablespoon of the oil in a pan and gently cook the onion for about 3 minutes. Add the garlic and spices and cook for a further 3 minutes.

In a pan of water boil the soya beans for 5 minutes or until cooked. Drain the beans and mash all the ingredients together with a potato masher. Alternatively, you could put all the ingredients into a blender or food-processor and pulse until coarse, not smooth.

Form the mixture into 8 patties, then set aside to rest for an hour or so. Heat the remaining tablespoon of oil in a non-stick frying pan and cook the bean burgers for about 5 minutes on each side.

*Good source of* Allium *vegetables and legumes. Source of soya*
PER PORTION: 274 KCAL, 11.3G FAT, 1.7G SATURATED FAT

# leek and butter bean crumble

This crumble makes for a wholesome and heart-warming meal which can be served with green leafy vegetables. This recipe has been kindly provided by Sylvia Wainwright.

SERVES 3

- 2 large leeks, sliced
- 1 garlic clove, crushed
- 4 tomatoes, roughly chopped
- 1 tablespoon rapeseed oil
- 400g tin butter beans, drained
- salt and pepper

**For the Topping**
- 100g wholemeal breadcrumbs
- 40g Brazil nuts, chopped
- 60g half-fat Cheddar cheese, grated

Preheat the oven to 180°C/350°F/gas 4.

Sauté the chopped leeks, garlic and tomatoes in the oil until soft. Blend half the butter beans to a paste and add to the mixture. Season and add the remaining whole beans.

Transfer the mixture to an ovenproof dish and top with the combined breadcrumbs, nuts and cheese. Cook in the oven for approximately 35–40 minutes.

*Good source of Allium vegetables, legumes and selenium. Source of lycopene and vitamin E*
PER PORTION: 411 KCAL, 18.5G FAT, 5.2G SATURATED FAT

# butter bean casserole with cider

Serve this casserole with chunky wholemeal bread to mop up the delicious sauce. This dish has been selected from *The New Cranks Recipe Book* by Nadine Abensur.

SERVES 6

- 500g butter beans
- 400g onions, diced
- 3 garlic cloves, crushed
- 100ml olive oil
- 250g carrots, cut into 2.5cm chunks
- dash of tamari (wheat-free soy sauce)
- 100ml cider
- 250g courgettes, cut into 2.5cm chunks
- 150g button mushrooms
- 250g sweetcorn kernels
- handful of fresh basil
- handful of fresh coriander
- salt and freshly ground black pepper

Boil the butter beans in plenty of water until they are tender but still intact. Meanwhile, sauté the onions and garlic in heated olive oil until pale gold in colour. Add the chunks of carrot and continue to sauté for a minute or 2, adding a little tamari and some of the cider. Then add the courgettes and sauté for a further minute without allowing them to lose their colour. Add the mushrooms, sauté for a few minutes, adding a little more tamari and a little more cider as well as salt and pepper to taste. Finally add the sweetcorn and continue to stir.

Add the cooked butterbeans with a little of the liquid they were cooked in and simmer gently for a further 10 minutes, adding the remaining cider so that all the flavours come together.

Mix with plenty of fresh chopped basil and coriander and serve.

*Good source of Allium vegetables and legumes*
PER PORTION: 460 KCAL, 18.8G FAT, 2.8G SATURATED FAT

# sarah's pad thai

Pad Thai ('Thai-style frying') is a well-known Thai dish which is also very popular outside of Thailand. This version provides an alternative way to enjoy cruciferous and *Allium* vegetables by combining them with traditional Thai flavours. This recipe has been kindly provided by Sarah Dilley.

SERVES 4

- 2 tablespoons rapeseed oil
- 3 eggs, beaten
- black pepper
- 250g tofu, cut into 2cm cubes
- 4 garlic cloves, finely chopped
- 1 large red chilli (optional)
- 400g bok choy and/or other greens, chopped
- 50g spring onions, cut into 3cm strips
- 400g pre-cooked rice noodles
- 200g bean sprouts
- handful of peanuts
- lime wedges to serve

*For the Sauce*
- 3 tablespoons oyster sauce
- 2 tablespoons fish sauce
- 2 tablespoons light soy sauce
- 1 tablespoon dark soy sauce (optional), plus extra to serve
- 1 tablespoon sugar

To make the sauce, simply combine all the sauce ingredients and set aside. Heat 1 tablespoon of the oil in a wok over a high heat. Add the beaten eggs and pepper and swirl the pan so that the egg covers the base of it. Continue to swirl the pan and cook for about 3 minutes until the egg forms an omelette.

Slide a spatula around the side of the omelette to lift it from the sides of the pan, then flip it over – don't worry if it breaks. Transfer the omelette to a plate and chop into small pieces. Heat the second tablespoon of oil in the wok over a medium–high heat. Stir-fry the tofu, garlic and chilli for 2 minutes. Add the bok choy or greens and the spring onions and stir-fry for a further 3 minutes.

Add the pre-cooked noodles and toss for 1 minute. Add the sauce and toss for a minute, then add the bean sprouts, chopped egg and peanuts and stir through. Serve with a lime wedge and dark soy sauce.

*Good source of Allium and cruciferous vegetables. Source of legumes, soya and vitamin E.*
PER PORTION: 418 KCAL, 18.2G FAT, 2.3G SATURATED FAT

# red lentil and caramelised onion and cabbage parcels

This lovely lunch dish was created by John Walter, Head Chef at the University of Surrey's Lakeside Restaurant. Serve the cabbage parcels with a crunchy side salad and Peanut and Linseed Bread (page 76).

SERVES 4

- 100g red lentils
- 8 large Savoy cabbage leaves
- 1 large onion, halved and sliced
- 2 teaspoons olive oil
- 2 teaspoons demerara sugar
- grated zest and juice of half a lemon
- freshly ground sea salt and black pepper

Preheat the oven to 180°C/350°F/gas 4.

Wash the lentils, put them in a lidded saucepan and cover with cold water. Bring to the boil and skim off any foam. Boil rapidly for 10 minutes, stirring from time to time, then reduce the heat to a simmer. Simmer for approximately 15 minutes, stirring and checking they are not burning or catching on the bottom of the pan. The resulting consistency should be like porridge.

Wash and then blanch the cabbage leaves in boiling water for 2 minutes only, then refresh them in ice-cold water and leave to drain. Sauté the onion slices in olive oil on a moderate heat. When they start to brown, add the sugar and stir until nicely caramelised.

Combine the onions, cooked lentils, lemon juice and zest, and season to taste. Pat dry the cabbage leaves and put a heaped spoonful of the filling in the middle near the base of each leaf. Fold over the sides of the cabbage leaf and roll them up.

Put the cabbage parcels seam sides down in an oiled baking dish and brush lightly with olive oil. Bake for 20–25 minutes until lightly browned.

*Source of Allium vegetables, cruciferous vegetables and legumes*
PER PORTION: 140 KCAL, 2.6G FAT, 0.4G SATURATED FAT

# pasta primavera

This pasta dish topped with a tasty vegetable sauce makes a filling lunch or evening meal. It has been adapted from a recipe in *Body and Beauty Foods* by Hazel Courteney and Kathryn Marsden.

SERVES 4

- 2 carrots, diced
- 2 courgettes, sliced
- 225g small broccoli florets
- 115g asparagus spears, cut into 2.5cm lengths
- 175g frozen peas
- 6–8 spring onions, chopped
- 2 garlic cloves, crushed
- 400g tin chopped tomatoes
- 150ml vegetable stock
- salt and pepper
- 1 tablespoon fresh parsley, chopped
- 1 tablespoon fresh basil, chopped
- 350g wholewheat pasta spirals
- grated Parmesan cheese, to serve (optional)

Put the carrots, courgettes, broccoli, asparagus, peas, spring onions, garlic, tomatoes and stock in a saucepan and bring to the boil, stirring occasionally. Reduce the heat, cover and simmer for 10 minutes, stirring occasionally.

Uncover and cook for a further 5–10 minutes until the vegetables are tender. Season to taste and stir in the herbs.

Meanwhile, cook the pasta according to the packet instructions and drain. Spoon the pasta on to plates and top with the sauce and a little Parmesan cheese if desired.

*Source of* **Allium** *vegetables, cruciferous vegetables, legumes, lycopene and vitamin E*
PER PORTION: 395 KCAL, 4.2G FAT, 0.9G SATURATED FAT

# potato-pastry quiche

The potato pastry in this quiche is a surprisingly flavoursome, low-fat alternative to regular pastry. The quiche can be made with roasted or fried vegetables. You could experiment with different vegetables, but ensure you pick some from the lists of beneficial foods. Serve with a leafy green salad. This recipe has been kindly provided by Kay Ford.

SERVES 4–6

*For the Potato Pastry*
- 500g potatoes (mixture of white and sweet), peeled and chopped
- 25g olive spread
- 55g cornflour

*For the Filling*
- 1 tablespoon olive oil
- 1 medium onion, red or white
- 3 garlic cloves, chopped
- 100g broccoli, chopped into small florets
- ½ red chilli, chopped
- ½ medium-size courgette, sliced
- 50g frozen peas
- 50g frozen sweetcorn
- 100g sliced mushrooms
- 5 eggs, beaten
- 50ml milk (soya milk)
- salt and pepper
- 1 tablespoon tomato purée
- 1 medium tomato, sliced
- dash of blue cheese (optional)

Preheat the oven to 180°C/350°F/gas 4.

Boil the potatoes for approximately 20 minutes or until soft. Drain and mash with the olive spread and cornflour. Grease a flan case and line with the mash mixture. Bake in the oven for 30–40 minutes. Set aside and leave to cool for at least an hour to allow the pastry to set. (You could cook the pastry a day in advance.)

Heat the oil in a frying pan over a medium heat and fry all the vegetables except the tomato for 5 minutes. Meanwhile beat the eggs together with the milk, salt and pepper.

Spread the tomato purée evenly over the potato pastry, fill the flan case with the vegetables and pour the egg mixture over them. Place the tomato slices over the quiche filling and dot the blue cheese, if using, on top. Return to the oven for a further 30 minutes.

*Good source of* **Allium** *vegetables. Source of cruciferous vegetables, lycopene, selenium, vitamin D and vitamin E*
PER PORTION: 409 KCAL, 18.7G FAT, 4.9G SATURATED FAT

# cauliflower curry

This recipe was kindly provided by TV Chef Gino D'Acampo. Here's what he has to say about it:

*'I have to admit that I'm not a big fan of curry, probably because it contains too many flavours and I'm not used to it, but whenever I have one, I tend to go for something mild and mainly vegetable based. Cauliflower works perfectly with the flavour of the curry paste, and the sweetness of the coconut milk balances the dish beautifully. I've tried this recipe with mixed vegetables and potatoes and it's fantastic.'*

SERVES 4

- 3 tablespoons olive oil
- 2 onions, finely chopped
- 1cm piece ginger, peeled and grated
- 3 tablespoons curry paste
- 400g tin coconut milk
- 400g tin chopped tomatoes
- 1 cauliflower, broken into pieces
- 2 potatoes, peeled and cut into 2cm chunks
- 3 tablespoons freshly squeezed lemon juice
- 200g spinach leaves, washed
- salt to taste

Heat the oil in a large saucepan and fry the onions for 5 minutes over a medium heat until softened, stirring occasionally. Add the ginger and curry paste and continue to fry for 3 more minutes, stirring continuously.

Pour in the coconut milk and the chopped tomatoes and bring to a simmer. Add the cauliflower and the potatoes and cook for about 25 minutes or until the potatoes are softened. Season with salt and remove the saucepan from the heat.

Add the lemon juice and spinach, cover and leave for 2 minutes. Serve hot, just as it is, or to accompany one of your favourite main courses.

*Good source of cruciferous vegetables. Source of Allium vegetables, lycopene and vitamin E*
PER PORTION: 301 KCAL, 14.8G FAT, 2.0G SATURATED FAT

# dr john's omelette

This is best served with green vegetables or a green salad. You can also grate a small amount of cheese into the beaten eggs or add a handful of fresh chopped basil with the tomatoes. This recipe has been kindly provided by Dr John Rayman.

SERVES 2

- 4 medium onions, or more to taste
- 1 tablespoon olive oil
- 12 cherry tomatoes, halved, or more to taste
- 5 eggs
- 2 tablespoons milk or soya milk
- handful of chopped chives (optional)

Preheat the grill to hot.

Chop the onions and fry gently in olive oil until soft and golden. Add the tomatoes and cook until just soft. Beat the eggs and milk in a bowl and add to the contents of the pan.

Cook gently, running a knife around the edge of the egg mixture to loosen it and allow the liquid to run underneath. When the eggs are half cooked, put the frying pan under the hot grill until the omelette has browned. Garnish with chives if desired.

*Good source of Allium vegetables. Source of lycopene, selenium, vitamin D and vitamin E*
PER PORTION: 414 KCAL, 24.5G FAT, 6.0G SATURATED FAT

# vegetarian chilli

The use of Quorn makes for a delicious vegetarian alternative to beef in this classic Mexican-style dish. Serve with rice or crusty bread and 'Chop-it-up' (Kushumb'r) (page 147).

SERVES 6

- 1 tablespoon olive oil
- 1 medium–large onion, finely chopped
- 4 garlic cloves, finely chopped
- 1 tablespoon cumin
- 1 teaspoon ground coriander
- 1 red chilli, finely chopped, or to taste
- 300g frozen Quorn mince
- 2 x 400g tins chopped tomatoes
- 400g tin baked beans
- 400g tin red kidney beans, drained
- salt and pepper
- ½ bunch of fresh coriander, roughly chopped

Heat the oil in a large lidded pan over a medium heat, add the onion and cook for 2–3 minutes. Add the garlic, spices and chilli and cook gently for a further 3 minutes.

Stir in the frozen Quorn mince and 2–3 tablespoons of water and cook gently for about 5 minutes. Stir in the tomatoes, baked beans, kidney beans and seasoning.

Place the lid on the pan and simmer for 15 minutes, stirring occasionally. Finally, stir in the fresh coriander and serve.

**Good source of Allium *vegetables, legumes and lycopene***
PER PORTION: 192 KCAL, 5.2G FAT, 0.7G SATURATED FAT

# stuffed peppers

The peanuts give this dish a lovely nutty flavour. Other grains such as bulgar wheat or rice can be used for the stuffing. A sprinkle of strong cheese in the last ten minutes of cooking adds a tasty topping. This dish has been kindly provided by Tracy Forward.

SERVES 2

- 75g couscous
- 200ml boiling water
- 2 large peppers
- 1 tablespoon olive oil, plus a little extra for drizzling
- 1 large onion, chopped
- 1 garlic clove, chopped
- 25g sun-dried tomatoes in oil, drained and chopped
- 25g unsalted peanuts
- 1 tablespoon sunflower seeds
- 2 large handfuls of rocket
- 1–2 tablespoons sweet chilli sauce

Preheat the oven to 180°C/350°F/gas 4.

Put the couscous in a saucepan and pour over the boiling water. Bring back to the boil and cook for a minute while stirring. Turn off the heat and leave the couscous to swell for about 5 minutes.

Cut the peppers in half through the stalks, remove the seeds and place them in an ovenproof dish. Gently heat the oil in a frying pan and cook the onion and garlic for about 5 minutes until golden brown. Add the tomatoes, peanuts and sunflower seeds and continue cooking for 1 minute.

Stir in the rocket and cook for a minute or so until it has wilted. Stir in the prepared couscous and chilli sauce to taste. Pile the mixture into the pepper halves, press down and drizzle with a little extra olive oil. Cover and cook for about 45 minutes or until the peppers are tender. Remove the cover for the last 10 minutes of cooking.

**Good source of Allium *vegetables. Source of cruciferous vegetables, lycopene and vitamin E***
PER PORTION: 526 KCAL, 34.9G FAT, 4.9G SATURATED FAT

# simple tomato sauce

This versatile sauce can be used with pasta, meat, poultry, fish or vegetables. It can be made with dried mixed herbs instead of fresh basil – just add two teaspoons when cooking the onion and garlic. The sauce can be blended to a smooth consistency if you prefer.

SERVES 4

- 1 tablespoon olive oil
- 1 large onion, finely chopped
- 4 garlic cloves, crushed
- 2 x 400g tins chopped tomatoes
- 4 tablespoons tomato purée
- 2 teaspoons sugar
- handful of fresh basil, chopped

Heat the oil in a saucepan and gently cook the onion and garlic until soft.

Add the tomatoes, tomato purée and sugar, and simmer for about 20 minutes adding a little water if the mixture becomes too thick.

Add the fresh basil and cook for a further couple of minutes.

*Good source of* **Allium** *vegetables and lycopene. Source of vitamin E*
PER PORTION: 123 KCAL, 4.0G FAT, 1.0G SATURATED FAT

# broccoli and broad bean frittata

Frittatas are a great way of using up leftover vegetables to make a filling meal in minutes. Do include vegetables that are particularly beneficial.

SERVES 2

- 20g olive spread
- 1 medium onion, sliced
- 110g potato, boiled and sliced or diced
- 80g broccoli florets, cooked
- 25g kale, cooked
- 80g broad beans, cooked
- 4 eggs
- salt and pepper

Preheat the grill to hot.

Melt the spread in a frying pan. Add the onion and sauté until soft. Add the potato and continue cooking until golden brown.

Add the remaining vegetables and heat through. Meanwhile, whisk together the eggs and season with salt and pepper. Add the egg mixture to the vegetables and stir gently.

Leave the frittata to set for a minute or so, then place the frying pan under a hot grill to brown the top.

*Source of* **Allium** *and cruciferous vegetables, legumes, selenium, vitamin D and vitamin E*
PER PORTION: 329 KCAL, 19.9G FAT, 5.4G SATURATED FAT

# vegetable sides

# braised red cabbage

This colourful dish makes a wonderful sweet-and-sour accompaniment to poultry, pork or game. The flavour benefits from the long, slow cooking time. This dish has been adapted from a recipe by Jane Baxter.

SERVES 6

- 550g red cabbage, shredded
- 250g onions, finely chopped
- 2 cooking apples, peeled, cored and finely chopped
- 2 garlic cloves, finely chopped
- 75g currants
- 1 teaspoon ground allspice
- 1 tablespoon brown sugar
- 1 tablespoon red wine vinegar
- 1 tablespoon olive spread
- salt and pepper

Preheat the oven to 150°C/300°F/gas 2.

Arrange a layer of cabbage in the base of a large casserole dish. Add a layer of onions, apples, garlic, currants, spices, sugar and seasoning. Continue to alternate the layers until all the ingredients are used.

Pour over the wine vinegar and dot with the olive spread. Cover the dish with foil and bake slowly in the oven for 1½–2 hours.

***Good source of cruciferous vegetables. Source of* Allium *vegetables***
PER PORTION: 71KCAL, 2G FAT, 0.4G SATURATED FAT

# baked shallots

This side dish makes a great accompaniment to a roast dinner; it has been adapted from a recipe by Jane Baxter.

SERVES 6

- 500g shallots, peeled
- 1 tablespoon olive spread
- salt and pepper
- 1 tablespoon sugar
- 125ml red wine

Preheat the oven to150°C/300°F/gas 2.

Arrange the peeled shallots in a single layer in a shallow pan. Dot with the olive spread and season to taste. Cook over a medium heat until browned.

Sprinkle with sugar and cook until the sugar disappears. Add the red wine and bring to the boil and cover. Bake in the oven for about 15 minutes until tender.

***Good source of* Allium *vegetables***
PER PORTION: 52 KCAL, 1.5G FAT, 0.3G SATURATED FAT

# moonblush tomatoes

This is one of Nigella Lawson's recipes. She invented it as a delicious alternative to buying sunblush tomatoes. The name refers to the way they are left to cook throughout the night. They can be served in any number of ways – with bread or cheese, as part of a salad or as a pasta sauce.

SERVES 5

- 500g (about 24) on-the-vine cherry or other baby tomatoes
- 2 teaspoons Maldon salt or 1 tablespoon table salt
- ¼ teaspoon sugar
- 1 teaspoon dried thyme
- 2 tablespoons olive oil

Preheat the oven to 220°C/425°F/gas 7.

Cut the tomatoes in half and sit them cut side up in an ovenproof dish. Sprinkle with the salt, sugar, thyme and olive oil. Put them in the oven and immediately turn it off. Leave the tomatoes in the oven overnight or for a whole day without opening the door.

*Source of lycopene*
PER PORTION: 66.8 KCAL, 5.6G FAT, 0.8G SATURATED FAT

# roasted tomatoes on the vine

Serving the tomatoes still on the vine makes an attractive and delicious side dish.

SERVES 2

- 200g cherry or other tomatoes on the vine
- 1 teaspoon olive oil
- salt and pepper

Preheat the oven to 200°C/400°F/gas 6.

Brush the tomatoes, still on the vine, with the olive oil and sprinkle with salt and pepper. Roast in the oven for 20–25 minutes.

*Source of lycopene*
PER PORTION: 32 KCAL, 1.9G FAT, 0.3G SATURATED FAT

# chop-it-up (kushumb'r)

Chop-it-up is named as such simply because that's all you need to do with each ingredient. It makes a refreshing chutney to accompany spicy dishes. This recipe has been kindly provided by Mrs John Dilley.

SERVES 4

- ½ cucumber
- 2 tomatoes
- 1 medium onion
- 1 tablespoon lime juice
- lettuce, shredded (optional)
- chilli, finely chopped (optional)

Dice the cucumber, tomatoes and onion by hand into cubes of uniform size and mix together. Stir in the lime juice and the lettuce and chilli, if using. You may remove the seeds and peel from the cucumber if you prefer.

*Source of Allium vegetables and lycopene*
PER PORTION: 29 KCAL, 0.3G FAT, 0.1G SATURATED FAT

# gujarati cabbage

This dish makes an ideal accompaniment to curries. Any type of cabbage will do, but Savoy is best. This dish has been adapted from a recipe by Jane Baxter.

SERVES 4

- 1 tablespoon vegetable oil
- 1 tablespoon black mustard seeds
- 1 dried chilli
- ½ cabbage, thinly sliced
- 2 carrots, coarsely grated
- 1 tablespoon sugar
- juice of half a lemon
- salt and pepper to taste

Heat the oil in a wok until hot and add the mustard seeds and chilli. When the seeds start to pop, add the cabbage and carrots and stir-fry for 5 minutes.

Add the remaining ingredients and season to taste. Cook for a further minute and serve immediately.

***Good source of cruciferous vegetables***
PER PORTION: 108 KCAL, 4.3G FAT, 0.5G SATURATED FAT

# dhal

This delicious dhal is lovely with naan bread or rice. Alternatively, it can be served as an accompaniment to your favourite curry.

SERVES 4

- 2 tablespoons olive oil
- 1 medium onion, chopped
- 3 garlic cloves, crushed
- 1 red chilli pepper, sliced
- 1 teaspoon ground turmeric
- 3 teaspoons garam masala
- 1 teaspoon cumin seeds
- 1cm piece fresh ginger
- 300g split red lentils, rinsed
- 2 medium tomatoes, chopped
- 2 tablespoons fresh coriander, chopped
- salt and pepper

Heat the oil in a large saucepan and gently cook the onion, garlic and chilli pepper until they just start to brown. Add the turmeric, garam masala, cumin seeds and ginger, and cook for a further 2 minutes.

Add the lentils and pour on 1 litre of boiling water. Bring the lentils to the boil and simmer for 15–20 minutes or until they are soft.

Add the tomatoes and cook for a further 5 minutes. Stir in the coriander, season to taste and serve.

*Good source of Allium vegetables and legumes. Source of lycopene*
PER PORTION: 337 KCAL, 8.8G FAT, 1.2G SATURATED FAT

# chickpea mash

Chickpea mash is a great alternative to mashed potato which can be ready in five minutes.

SERVES 2

- 400g tin chickpeas, drained
- black pepper
- 1 dessertspoon olive oil
- 1 tablespoon chopped fresh parsley

Gently heat the drained chickpeas in a pan of water over a low heat for a few minutes and drain. There is no need to boil them as they are already cooked.

Grind in the pepper to taste and mash the chickpeas with a potato masher. Finally, stir in the olive oil and parsley.

*Good source of legumes*
PER PORTION: 180 KCAL, 8.0G FAT, 1.0G SATURATED FAT

# moros y cristianos (black beans with white rice)

This recipe is another reminder of the Moors' place in Spanish history, a visual as well as a culinary reference with the black beans and white rice. Moros y Cristianos can be served with roast duck. This recipe was taken from *Moro: The Cookbook* by Sam and Sam Clark.

SERVES 4

- 150g black beans, soaked overnight
- ½ medium onion
- 2 garlic cloves
- 2 bay leaves, preferably fresh
- ½ cinnamon stick
- juice and zest of half an orange
- 3 tablespoons olive oil
- ½ small bunch of fresh flat-leaf parsley, roughly chopped
- 150g white rice (Calasparra)
- sea salt and black pepper

Drain the beans and place in a large saucepan with at least 6 times their volume of cold water. Add the onion, garlic, bay leaves and cinnamon stick.

Scoop off any foam that forms on the top and cook for 1–2 hours until soft. Season with salt and pepper, add the orange zest, orange juice, olive oil and parsley and set aside.

Simmer the rice in lightly salted boiling water until firm but not chalky (about 10–15 minutes) and drain. When you are ready, serve the rice, then spoon the beans and a little of their juices on top so you can see both the black and white.

*Good source of legumes. Source of Allium vegetables*
PER PORTION: 359 KCAL, 10.6G FAT, 1.5G SATURATED FAT

# broccoli saltati

This Italian-style broccoli stir-fry was kindly provided by Gino D'Acampo. Here is what he has to say about it:

*'Everybody in my family loves broccoli and we always have it in the house. One day I thought I would experiment with a few oriental ingredients. This is what came out of that day.'*

SERVES 6

- 5 tablespoons olive oil
- 2 tablespoons runny honey
- 1 tablespoon light soy sauce
- 2 tablespoons balsamic vinegar
- 1 garlic clove, finely sliced
- 1 small red chilli, deseeded and finely sliced
- 3 tablespoons sliced fresh basil leaves
- 60g pine nuts
- 700g broccoli, cut into florets
- salt and pepper

Mix together 1 tablespoon of the olive oil, the honey, soy sauce, balsamic vinegar, garlic, chilli, basil and pine nuts in a large bowl.

Bring a large saucepan of salted water to the boil and cook the broccoli for 3 minutes until *al dente*. Drain the broccoli and place in the bowl with the dressing. Toss gently to avoid breaking up the broccoli.

Heat the remaining olive oil in a wok and fry the broccoli with the dressing for 4 minutes until piping hot, stirring frequently. Adjust seasoning and serve as an accompaniment to fish or meat.

**Good source of cruciferous vegetables. Source of vitamin E**
PER PORTION: 240 KCAL, 19.6G FAT, 2.4G SATURATED FAT

# sweet potato boulangère

Sweet potatoes make a great change to ordinary potatoes in this classic dish.

SERVES 6

- 900g sweet potatoes, peeled and sliced
- 1 large onion, peeled and sliced
- 3 garlic cloves, crushed
- 600ml hot chicken stock
- 1 teaspoon dried mixed herbs
- 1 teaspoon dried thyme

Preheat the oven to 200°C/400°F/gas 6.

Put the potatoes, onion and garlic into a large saucepan and pour over the hot stock. Add the herbs and bring to the boil for 10 minutes.

Pour into an ovenproof dish and place in the oven for about 45 minutes or until there is only a small amount of liquid left.

**Good source of Allium vegetables. Source of vitamin E**
PER PORTION: 152 KCAL, 0.9G FAT, 0.2G SATURATED FAT

desserts

# berry and nut crumble

This is a delicious crumble with a wonderfully different topping. To make it a source or good source of the particularly beneficial polyphenols, simply substitute raspberries for some or all of the mixed berries.

SERVES 6

- 500g frozen mixed berries, defrosted
- 3 tablespoons sugar

**For the Crumble Topping**
- 115g plain flour
- 115g soya spread
- 115g porridge oats
- 55g Brazil nuts, chopped
- 90g sugar
- pinch of salt

Preheat the oven to 200°C/400°F/gas 6.

Put the fruit into an ovenproof dish and sprinkle with the sugar.

Put the flour into a bowl and rub in the spread until it resembles fine breadcrumbs. Add the remaining ingredients and mix well.

Spread the crumble mixture over the fruit and bake for about 30 minutes or until the top is golden.

*Good source of selenium. Source of vitamin D and vitamin E*
PER PORTION: 418 KCAL, 19.6G FAT, 4.7G SATURATED FAT

# winter fruit salad

This is a wonderful, warm dessert which tastes excellent with a little soya ice cream. You could try varying the dried fruit. This recipe has been kindly provided by Sylvia Wainwright.

SERVES 6

- 250g prunes
- 250g dried apricots
- 250g dried peaches
- 2 cooking apples, peeled and sliced
- 2 green tea bags

Place all the ingredients in a pan. Add barely enough water to cover the fruit and simmer for approximately 10 minutes.

Allow to cool and remove the tea bags.

*Source of polyphenols*
PER PORTION: 254 KCAL, 0.9G FAT, 0.0G SATURATED FAT

# pomegranate upside-down cake

This is a new take on an old classic and is perfect for a cold autumn afternoon with a warm cup of green tea

SERVES 8

*For the Topping*
- 475ml pomegranate juice
- 300g pomegranate arils
- 25g sugar

*For the Sponge*
- 175g olive spread
- 175g sugar
- 3 eggs
- 175g self-raising flour, sifted
- 3 tablespoons milk
- 2 tablespoons of orange or lemon juice or a teaspoon of vanilla extract

Preheat the oven to 180°C/350°F/gas 4.

Gently reduce the pomegranate juice in a non-stick pan with a large base over a low–medium heat until it turns into syrup. Stir occasionally and do not allow to boil as this will cause the sugars to caramelise and set hard. As the juice reduces, adjust the heat accordingly, until there are only about 4 or 5 tablespoons left; this will take up to about 50 minutes.

Meanwhile, make the sponge. Cream the olive spread and sugar together in a large mixing bowl. Whisk in the eggs with a couple of tablespoons of the flour. Then fold in the remaining flour. Finally mix in the milk and fruit juice or vanilla extract.

Line a cake tin (20cm diameter) with greaseproof paper. Ladle in the pomegranate syrup and spread evenly over the base. Sprinkle over the sugar then cover with all but a handful of the arils in an even layer. Spoon the cake batter over the fruit and smooth the top. Bake in the oven for 45–50 minutes or until cooked through (test by sticking a skewer into the middle – it should come out clean). Leave the cake to cool for 5 minutes.

Tip the cake out on to a rack and cool for a further 20 minutes. Upside-down cake is best served when still warm. Sprinkle the reserved pomegranate arils around the plate to decorate.

*Good source of polyphenols*
PER PORTION: 378 KCAL, 16.6G FAT, 3.3G SATURATED FAT

# summer fruits in red wine, monbazillac, basil and mint

This wonderfully subtle recipe was kindly provided by chef Raymond Blanc's kitchen. It is perfect for a summer's day with the refreshing taste of red fruits combined with a hint of mint and basil. Other fruits can be used (blackberries, blueberries or peaches). If the fruit is not ripe enough you can marinate it in a little sugar for an hour. This dessert can be prepared 4–6 hours in advance.

SERVES 4

- 250ml Monbazillac or other dessert wine
- 100ml red wine (Cabernet Sauvignon)
- 40g caster sugar
- ½ vanilla pod, seeds scraped out and set aside
- 5g (12 leaves) fresh mint, lightly chopped
- 3g (6 leaves) fresh basil, lightly chopped

- 225g raspberries
- 160g strawberries, stemmed, halved and quartered
- 40g wild strawberries (optional)
- 1 large wedge of watermelon, peeled and diced or made into balls
- 100ml chilled pink champagne (optional, but the remainder will be very much appreciated by your guests)

Bring the two wines, sugar, vanilla pods and seeds to the boil in a pan. Boil to remove the alcohol and turn off the heat. Tie the herbs up in a muslin bag and add to the pan to infuse the liquid. Cool down to approximately 40°C so that the fruit does not cook and lose its shape.

Add the raspberries, strawberries and the melon and refrigerate for at least 4 hours.

Remove the herbs and vanilla pods and place the soup and fruit into a large serving bowl or 4 individual bowls. Pour approximately 2 tablespoons of the pink champagne, if using, over the top as you are serving.

*Good source of lycopene. Source of polyphenols*
PER PORTION: 193 KCAL, 0.5G FAT, 0.2G SATURATED FAT

# watermelon sorbet

This sorbet is a beautiful pink colour and has a refreshing taste.

SERVES 4

- 75ml pomegranate juice (or water)
- 75g caster sugar
- ½ watermelon
- juice of half a lemon

Heat the pomegranate juice or water and the sugar in a pan over a medium heat, stirring occasionally. Heat for a few minutes until the sugar has dissolved; there is no need to boil. Remove from the heat and chill in the fridge.

Remove and discard the seeds from the watermelon. Scoop out the flesh and whizz in a blender with the lemon juice until smooth. Mix the watermelon purée with the pomegranate and sugar mixture. Churn and freeze the sorbet mixture in an ice-cream maker following the manufacturer's instructions. Alternatively, pour into a freezer-proof container and place in the freezer. Leave for an hour, allowing the mixture to begin to freeze.

Remove from the freezer and mix with a whisk to break up the ice, then replace. Repeat this several times until the sorbet is frozen. This will take up to about 5 hours.

*Good source of lycopene*
PER PORTION: 122 KCAL, 0.4G FAT, 0.1G SATURATED FAT

# crêpes with raspberry sauce

These crêpes make an attractive dessert and are also ideal for a special breakfast.

SERVES 4

- 90g plain flour
- 1 egg, lightly beaten
- 250ml soya milk
- 20g olive spread, melted
- pinch of salt
- extra fat spread for greasing the pan

**For the Sauce**
- 500g raspberries
- 1 teaspoon brown sugar
- icing sugar for dusting

Place the flour in a large bowl and whisk in the egg, milk, fat spread and salt until the batter is smooth. Chill in the fridge for 1 hour.

Preheat the oven to 120°C/250°F/gas ½.

While the batter is chilling, set aside a few raspberries for each portion. Place half the remaining raspberries into a saucepan with a teaspoon of water and sprinkle over the teaspoon of sugar. Cook the raspberries over a medium heat for approximately 5 minutes, breaking them up with a wooden spoon. Reduce the heat and allow the sauce to thicken; this will take about 5 minutes.

Add the other half of the raspberries and gently heat until they are warmed through but whole. Grease a non-stick frying pan with a little spread and place over a medium heat. Ladle about 3 tablespoons of the batter into the pan and swirl it so that it is covered with a thin layer of batter. Cook for about a minute, running a spatula around the edge of the crêpe to lift it away from the edges. Shake the pan to loosen the crêpe and flip it over. When cooked, transfer to a plate and keep warm in the oven while you cook the rest of the crêpes.

Lay a crêpe on to a plate and spoon on some of the sauce. Fold a third from one side into the middle, then a third from the other side. Repeat until you have 8 crêpes. Dust with icing sugar and garnish with a few of the reserved raspberries.

**Good source of polyphenols. Source of soya**
PER PORTION: 215 KCAL, 9.0G FAT, 2.8G SATURATED FAT

# dairy-free chocolate ice cream

This delicious dessert was devised by John Walter, Head Chef at the University of Surrey's Lakeside Restaurant. He originally created it for his son who has a milk allergy. If you have a sweet tooth, go for a sweeter dark chocolate as some dark chocolate can be quite bitter.

SERVES 6

- 300g dairy-free dark chocolate, broken into squares, plus extra to garnish
- 500ml soya single cream alternative

Place both the chocolate and soya cream in a microwaveable bowl. Microwave on defrost for 3 minutes or until the chocolate has melted. Stir well.

Pour the mixture into a freezer-proof container and freeze for about 2 hours. Remove the ice cream from the freezer and whisk until smooth.

Return to the freezer for a couple of hours or until the ice cream has set. Scoop into bowls and add a piece of dark chocolate to serve.

*Source of soya*
PER PORTION: 367 KCAL, 26.8G FAT, 12.4G SATURATED FAT

# chocolate pots

These chocolate pots are smooth and creamy and blend beautifully with the fresh raspberries. The recipe has been selected from www.alprosoya.co.uk.

SERVES 4

- 100g luxury Belgian dark chocolate
- 12 white marshmallows, chopped
- 115g fresh raspberries
- 250ml chocolate-flavoured soya alternative to milk

Break the chocolate into squares, place in a bowl with the marshmallows and melt over a pan of hot water. Place sufficient raspberries in each ramekin dish to cover the base.

With a balloon whisk, combine the chocolate-flavoured milk alternative with the melted chocolate mixture and pour into the individual ramekins, over the raspberries.

Chill for 2 hours and serve decorated with a couple of fresh raspberries and a sprig of mint.

*Source of polyphenols and soya*
PER PORTION: 231 KCAL, 8.5G FAT, 4.5G SATURATED FAT

# ruby fruit salad with raspberry coulis

This is a pretty and refreshing dessert that is very simple to make.

SERVES 4

- 110g pomegranate arils
- 110g watermelon
- 110g red seedless grapes
- 110g raspberries

**For the Coulis**
- 130g raspberries
- juice of half a lime
- 3 tablespoons icing sugar

Combine the fruit and place in 1 large or 4 individual serving dishes.

Mix the raspberries with the lime juice and icing sugar and blend to make a smooth purée. Drizzle the coulis over the fruit and serve.

**Good source of polyphenols. Source of lycopene**
PER PORTION: 259 KCAL, 1.3G FAT, 0.3G SATURATED FAT

# pomegranate sorbet

The sharp, tangy flavours of the pomegranate and lime combine in this vibrant sorbet to make an irresistible dessert.

SERVES 4

- 75ml water
- 75ml sugar
- 475–500ml pomegranate juice
- juice of half a lime

Heat the water and sugar in a pan over a medium heat for a few minutes, stirring occasionally until the sugar has dissolved (there is no need to boil). Remove from the heat and chill in the fridge.

Mix the pomegranate and lime juices with the water and sugar mixture. Churn and freeze the sorbet mixture in an ice-cream maker following the manufacturer's instructions. Alternatively, pour into a freezer-proof container and place in the freezer.

Leave for an hour, allowing the mixture to begin to freeze. Remove from the freezer and mix with a whisk to break up the ice, then replace.

Repeat this several times until the sorbet is frozen. This will take up to 7 hours.

*Good source of polyphenols*
PER PORTION: 127 KCAL, 0.0G FAT, 0.0G SATURATED FAT

# raspberry and brazil nut muffins

These moreish muffins have a lovely nutty bite. They freeze well and can be gently warmed in the microwave.

MAKES 12 MUFFINS

- 2 medium eggs
- 175g sugar
- 60ml rapeseed oil
- 175ml soya milk
- 175g white flour, sifted
- 85g wholemeal flour, sifted
- 85g porridge oats
- 1 tablespoon baking powder
- 2 x 290g tins raspberries in fruit juice, drained
- 55g Brazil nuts, roughly chopped

Preheat the oven to 190°C/375°F/gas 5.

Place 12 muffin cases in a 12-cup muffin tin. Whisk together the eggs and sugar until pale and fluffy. Add the oil and milk and continue to whisk until incorporated. Add all the dry ingredients and fold in.

Finally, add the raspberries and Brazil nuts and fold in. Pour the mixture into the muffin cases and cook for 25–30 minutes until well risen and golden brown.

**Good source of selenium. Source of polyphenols**
PER MUFFIN: 262 KCAL, 10.4G FAT, 1.5G SATURATED FAT

# glossary

**5-alpha-dihydroxytestosterone:** A more potent product of the male sex hormone testosterone.

**Androgen receptor:** By binding to the androgen receptor, the androgen hormones, testosterone and dihydrotestosterone turn on genes to produce proteins that are responsible for male characteristics and control the behaviour of cells.

**Androgen-insensitive cells:** Cells that no longer react to androgens.

**Androgens:** A group of male sex hormones including testosterone and dihydrotestosterone.

**Anti-atherogenic:** Helps prevent atherosclerosis (see later entry).

**Antimicrobial:** A substance that either prevents the growth of or kills bacteria.

**Antioxidant:** A substance, such as vitamin E, vitamin C or beta-carotene, thought to protect body cells from the damaging effects of oxidation (see later entry).

**Atherosclerosis:** The build-up of fatty deposits in the arteries.

**Blood vessels:** Tubular vessels including arteries and veins that transport blood around the body.

**Cancer cells:** Cells that have become cancerous.

**Cell division:** A process whereby a cell divides into new cells.

**Detoxification:** The process of making a harmful substance less toxic.

**Diallyl disulphide (DADS):** An organosulphur compound produced by *Allium* vegetables.

**DNA:** Deoxyribonucleic acid – a double helix structure that contains the genetic information required to direct the development and functioning of all living organisms.

**Enzyme:** A protein that speeds up the rate of a chemical reaction.

**Estrogen receptor-beta:** A receptor located on DNA that is activated by oestrogen (estrogen) that can turn on genes regulating the production of proteins and resulting in a change in cell function.

**Fatty acid:** A basic component of fats and oils released during digestion. The type of fatty acid determines the properties of dietary fat (e.g. solid or oil) and the structure of cell membranes.

**Gene:** A section of DNA (genetic material) that provides the instructions for the creation of a specific protein.

**Gleason score:** A score (between two and ten) based upon the appearance of prostate tissue (how well organised it is) under the microscope; cancers with a higher Gleason score are more aggressive.

**Goitrogen:** A substance that inhibits the uptake of iodine from the diet and interferes with thyroid function.

**Hormone:** A substance that is made in one part of the body and is released into the bloodstream so that it can travel to the organs or body tissues and interact with an appropriate receptor; a hormone triggers a change in the structure or function of its target.

**Hormone-dependent disease:** Prostate cancer which requires androgens, particularly the hormone testosterone, in order to grow.

**Hormone-independent disease:** Prostate cancer which has adapted so that it no longer needs androgens in order to grow.

**Immune function:** A number of processes that help to protect the body from disease.

**Immune response:** The response of the body to a harmful invader, e.g. an infective agent or cancer cells.

**Inflammation:** A localised protective reaction of tissue to irritation, injury, or infection, characterised by pain, redness, swelling and sometimes loss of function.

**Insulin-like growth-factor-1:** A hormone that stimulates growth.

**Locally advanced disease:** Prostate cancer that has spread beyond the prostate gland into the surrounding tissue.

**Metabolite:** A product or intermediate product of a set of chemical reactions in the body.

**Metastatic:** When a cancer spreads from its original site to another area of the body it is called metastasis.

**Nutrients:** Substances that are typically eaten and provide the materials for growth and energy or help regulate these processes. Examples of macronutrients are carbohydrate, protein and fat, and examples of micronutrients are vitamins and minerals, such as vitamin C and selenium.

**Oestrogen (Estrogen):** A female sex hormone that promotes the formation of female characteristics.

**Oxidation:** An interaction with oxygen. PUFAs (polyunsaturated fatty acids) may undergo oxidation inside the body which, when excessive, may result in harmful effects.

**Oxidative stress:** A condition of increased oxidant production in animal cells characterised by the release of harmful substances that result in damage to cells.

**Pre-cancerous:** A condition that if left untreated may result in cancer.

**PSA:** Prostate Specific Antigen – a protein that is produced by the prostate gland and is often elevated in prostate cancer. Elevated PSA levels can be detected with a blood test and provide an indicator for prostate cancer diagnosis and progression.

**PSA doubling time:** The period of time that it takes for a PSA level to double. The shorter the doubling time, the more aggressive the cancer is likely to be, so it is used as an indicator of prostate cancer progression.

**Stage III or IV prostate cancer:** At stage III, cancer has spread beyond the outer layer of the prostate to nearby tissues. At stage IV, cancer has spread to other parts of the body, such as the bladder, rectum, bone, liver, lungs and lymph nodes.

**Status:** A description of deficiency, adequacy or excess of a nutrient.

**Testosterone:** A male sex hormone that promotes the formation of male characteristics.

**Tumour:** A swelling that is formed by the abnormal growth of cells such as cancer cells.

The following recipes and variations of recipes have been reprinted by kind permission:

**Porridge with raspberry and pomegranate compote:** adapted from a recipe on www.alprosoya.co.uk

**Bagels with oven-roasted tomatoes and rocket:** taken from www.eggrecipes.co.uk

**Watercress soup:** adapted from a recipe on www.alprosoya.co.uk

**POM salsa:** recipe selected from www.pomwonderful.com

**Tuna stir-fry:** adapted from a recipe on www.sainsburys.co.uk/food

**POM vinaigrette:** recipe from www.pomwonderful.com

**POM stuffed halibut:** adapted from a recipe on www.pomwonderful.com

**Turkey and apricot bake:** adapted from a recipe on www.sainsburys.co.uk/food

**Spicy bean pitta:** adapted from a recipe in Morrison's *Let's Eat Smart* magazine (January/February 2008)

**Baked shallots, Braised red cabbage, Gujarati cabbage:** adapted from recipes by Jane Baxter on www.riverford.co.uk

**Chocolate pots:** recipe selected from www.alprosoya.co.uk

The recipes and variations of recipes below have been selected from the following cookery books and reprinted by kind permission of the publishers:

From *Arabesque* by Claudia Roden, Penguin Books Limited, reprinted by kind permission of David Higham Associates:

**Prawns in spicy tomato sauce**
**Stuffed aubergine**

From *Body and Beauty Foods* by Hazel Courteney and Kathryn Marsden, published by Ivy Press:
**Pasta Primavera**
**Sweet and sour turkey meatballs**
**Tagliatelle with salmon, courgettes and almonds**

From *Cooking with the Kosher Butcher's Wife* by Sharon Lurie, published by Struik (2006):
**Liver and onions**

From *Gordon Ramsay Makes it Easy* by Gordon Ramsay, published by Quadrille (2005):
**Tiger prawn salad with mango and avocado**

From *Moro: the Cookbook* by Sam and Sam Clark, published by Ebury. Reprinted by permission of The Random House Group Ltd:
**Broad bean purée**
**Moros y cristianos**

From *Nigella Express* by Nigella Lawson, published by Chatto & Windus. Reprinted by permission of The Random House Group Ltd:
**Moonblush tomatoes**

From *The New Cranks Recipe Book* by Nadine Abensur, published by Weidenfeld & Nicolson, reprinted by kind permission from Cranks:
**Butter bean casserole**
**Caribbean pepperpot**
**Cauliflower and broccoli salad**

The following recipes were kindly provided by celebrity chefs. For further information see their websites, listed below:

Alex Mackay, www.alexmackay.com
**Tiger prawn and shiitake mushroom broth**
**Sea-bream with sunblush tomatoes and basil**

Antony Worrall Thompson, www.awtonline.co.uk
**Chilled tomato bisque**
**Spicy sardines with chickpea and avocado salad**

Cyrus Todiwala, www.cafespice.co.uk
**Saag aloo with oily fish**
**Stuffed duck breast (Badak chaanti badami pasanda)**
**Jardaloo ma murghi**

Gino D'Acampo, www.ginodacampo.com
**Cauliflower curry**
**Broccoli saltati**

Raymond Blanc, www.raymondblanc.com
**Summer fruits in red wine, Monbazillac, basil and mint**
**Poached salmon steak on spinach and watercress purée**

Details of the University of Surrey's Lakeside Restaurant can be found on: www.som.surrey.ac.uk/about/lakeside/index.asp Head chef John Walter kindly provided the following recipes:

**Devilled mackerel with tomato and mint salad**
**Trout and leek paupiette in carrot and coriander sauce**
**Red lentil and caramelised onion and cabbage parcels**
**Dairy-free ice cream**

The following recipes were provided by Dr John Rayman (additional recipes credited throughout the book):

**Dr John's meatballs**
**Stir-fried pork fillet**
**Peanut and linseed bread**

# index

# further information

The recommendations given in this book are a guideline to the types and quantities of foods that we feel may have the potential to reduce the risk or progression of prostate cancer. These foods should be eaten as part of a balanced diet that provides a wide variety of foods and nutrients. For further information on eating a balanced diet please refer to the Food Standards Agency website at www.eatwell.gov.uk.

For further information on cancer, and specifically prostate cancer, the following websites may be helpful:
- Prostate Cancer Research Foundation: www.thepcrf.org.uk
- The Prostate Cancer Charity: www.prostate-cancer.org.uk
- Cancer Research UK: www.cancerhelp.org.uk
- Macmillan Cancer Support/Cancer Backup: www.cancerbackup.org.uk

**Would you like to help with our research?**
Researchers at the Food, Consumer Behaviour and Health Research Centre at the University of Surrey are interested in your views on food, prostate health and how you view this cookbook. Please log on to our website (www.fahs.surrey.ac.uk/survey/prostatecarecookbook/) and complete a short questionnaire.